T0318416

"You might ask yourself, how did we get here: broken public services, polluted rivers and the return of rickets? Chris Grocott provides a crucial part of the answer, deftly recounting the history of the ideas that have come to drive policy, shape behaviour and dominate thinking."
David Harvie, *co-author of* Shaping for Mediocrity:
The Cancellation of Critical Thinking at Our Universities,
and co-editor of Commoning *with George Caffentzis and Silvia Federici*

"The state of affairs that economists so often justify is producing gigantic inequalities and a climate crisis. In this beautiful little book, Chris Grocott punctures the old stories and encourages the birth of new ones. This is essential reading which will help us to produce a low carbon, high inclusion, high democracy economy."
Martin Parker, *Professor of Organization Studies,*
University of Bristol Business School, UK

THE IDEAS THAT RULE US

It may seem surprising that the economic choices we make in society are often determined by ideas rather than scientific evidence or financial resources. The consequences of such choices are often stark – such as the austerity policies which eroded our ability to withstand crises like the Covid-19 pandemic. This book explores the ideas that rule how our economy works, how government operates, and how workers organise.

A small number of historical economic ideas remain stubbornly prevalent and powerful today. However, they are largely based on questionable assumptions about human behaviour and unproven theoretical ideas about economics. They were founded within the realms of philosophy and politics rather than hard science. This book illustrates how politicians have selectively borrowed convenient economic concepts in order to promote and defend policies which entrench and escalate inequalities and other structural problems.

This accessible book invites readers to question the ideas that rule us and explore the challenges facing society. It invites progressive thought about how we need to urgently organise action for the future.

Chris Grocott is Lecturer in Management and Economic History at the University of Leicester, UK.

THE IDEAS THAT RULE US

How to Understand, Organise, and Fight Against Bad Economics

Chris Grocott

Routledge
Taylor & Francis Group

LONDON AND NEW YORK

Designed cover image: retrorocket / iStock / Getty Images Plus

First published 2025
by Routledge
4 Park Square, Milton Park, Abingdon, Oxon OX14 4RN

and by Routledge
605 Third Avenue, New York, NY 10158

Routledge is an imprint of the Taylor & Francis Group, an informa business

British Library Cataloguing in Publication Data
A catalogue record for this book is available from the British Library

Library of Congress Cataloging-in-Publication Data
A catalog record has been requested for this book

ISBN: 9780367753146 (hbk)
ISBN: 9780367753139 (pbk)
ISBN: 9781003161950 (ebk)

DOI: 10.4324/9781003161950

Typeset in Sabon
by Taylor & Francis Books

CONTENTS

ACKNOWLEDGEMENTS

I'm grateful to Jo Grady for working with me to put together the original proposal for this volume. And to Terry Clague, commissioning editor at Routledge, who has been very supportive and encouraging of this project.

Thanks to Christie Dimitropoulou, David Harvie, Sylvia Reid, Gareth Stockey, and Becky Talbott for very helpful comments and feedback on the first draft of this manuscript. Thanks also to Nuala Harvey who gave the manuscript a fierce copyediting.

Thank you to my parents and friends for their support during the writing of this book. Begun on the eve of the Covid pandemic, the challenges to its production have been far from solely academic. In particular, I am grateful to my partner Becky for love, support, and encouragement throughout.

Small but forthright in expressing her opinions on a range of subjects, special mention should go to Hoppy the dog.

1

INTRODUCTION

For centuries, who should have access to what in the economy, how they should access it, and why they should be given access to it, have been debated fiercely. Key to this debate is the question of how our economy should be organised. For a brief period between 1945 and 1979, 'good' economics addressed itself to how, through collective endeavour, we could manage our resources to create a fairer society. But, for a century and a half before that, and still ongoing today, 'good' economics, the kind taught in academic Economics departments, has based itself on the idea that, rather than through collective effort, it is through individuals striving to enrich themselves that beneficial economic growth will occur.[1] Yet, having organised our economy around that idea, we have issues still to solve. To name but a few there are: unemployment; fuel, and other kinds of, poverty; and gross inequalities in incomes across countries, genders, and ethnicities.

This book charts the rise of the idea that 'good' economics means that we cannot solve inequality, economic unfairness, or poverty. It does so by looking at the everyday economic ideas used by politicians, and in common currency all around us. Those suggest that collective attempts to improve society are a utopian dream, that they are 'bad' economics, and that they will result in society being poorer and in the infringement of the personal liberty of individuals. We look at the origins of that idea and at the ideas that challenge it. We do so because the

DOI: 10.4324/9781003161950-1

issue is not a simple, practical one around what 'good' or 'bad' economics is; rather, it is one of ideas. As the political economist John Maynard Keynes put it, when it comes to ideas 'we are ruled by little else'.[2] Even the most practical people are 'usually the slave of some long defunct economist'.[3] In this book, we identify and examine the ideas that rule us.

What is the Point of Economics?

Before setting out to see how mainstream economics has been used by politicians and other commentators to favour individual over collective solutions to economic problems, it makes sense to look at what economists, who study our daily economic lives, understand our reality to be. That our daily life bears little resemblance to the economist's world might well begin to explain some major questions, such as why most economists did not predict the global crisis of 2007–2008 and the subsequent 'Great Recession', an issue we address in Chapter Thirteen.

In everyday life, whenever you buy or sell something, you are engaged in a deceptively simple process – one person offers a good or service, whilst the other offers money. But behind this simple transaction is an ornate architecture of economic ideas that govern what is available to whom and for what price. Most academic economists see economics as being a discipline devoted to the understanding of the distribution of scarce resources in our society. Mainstream economics believes that we cannot afford to do everything we would like to in society because our resources are scarce. Let us explore what mainstream economics does with its scarce resources.

Mainstream economics has, at its heart, the law of supply and demand, by which resources are distributed within the economy.[4] In theory, this can be understood by thinking of two people, one with a good or service to sell, the other with something to give in exchange. Oddly enough, this isn't normally thought of by economists in terms of hard cash. It's assumed that someone who wants to sell, say, cows and someone who wants to sell cheese will work out between them how many cows and cheeses they need to exchange to get the job done. Which is odd, given that you don't see people trying that one in supermarkets.

The question of how many cows your cheese buys you comes down to how much supply or demand there is for those products. When something is in greater supply than demand, its price will lower. When demand is higher than supply, its price will rise. Buyers and sellers agree a price based upon their knowledge of the supply and demand of a product. At the point at which buyer and seller agree a price relative to supply and demand, the market reaches what we call an equilibrium and clears, i.e. sells out.[5] The cycle is repeated millions, perhaps billions of times a day as we go about our daily lives buying and selling goods and services, or when we do not spend because we do not like the price set.

For the laws of supply and demand to work properly, however, you need to make two assumptions about human nature. The first is that people have access to what is called perfect market information. In other words, people always have enough information to know the prices at which goods and services should be charged. The second is the idea that people are rational economic agents, which is to say that they seek to always maximise their returns. Almost no other assumptions about human nature are made in mainstream economics.

A problem that we will return to throughout this book is that people rarely, if ever, have perfect market information, and that people don't always seek to maximise their returns.[6] Take, for example, the toilet roll crisis of 2020 in Britain, where people who were fearful of the coming lockdown flocked to supermarkets to buy toilet roll, leaving bereft shelves and a national shortage. In March 2020, two behavioural researchers, Liam Smith and Celine Klemm, wrote in the *Guardian* that despite understanding the psychology of panic buying and rationally knowing that the country was not going to run out or ban trips for buying it, they nevertheless ended up stockpiling toilet roll themselves.[7] They argued that people did this because of expressions of panic on social media platforms, which then caused anxiety in those who had not stockpiled, and because, in the face of a pandemic about which individuals could not do much, stockpiling felt like taking back some control. Rational, this most certainly was not, even if it was understandable.

Likewise, the petrol shortage of 2021. At petrol stations throughout Britain, queues formed, some stretching half a mile or more, with people trying to fill up their tanks for the week's commute ahead.[8] Oddly though, this was sparked by a couple of supermarket chains running low on stocks, rather than a universal shortage, and, crucially, by Boris Johnson assuring the country there was nothing to panic about. Now, of course you can argue that believing the opposite of anything the then Prime Minister tells you is rational. But, nevertheless, people were given a very accurate appraisal of the stock of petrol and chose to ignore it. The unintended consequence was that petrol stations did start selling out as the panic buying continued. Even then, there remained plenty of petrol in the country; the problem was supplying it quickly to those areas where it was selling out fastest. By contrast, in March 2022, at the Treasury Select Committee, the economist Amrita Sen predicted that the Russia–Ukraine war could spike petrol to a high of 250p per litre.[9] A few local petrol stations sold out as some people engaged in panic buying, but this time, despite good reason to fill up sooner rather than later, people generally did not.

Mainstream economics makes basic assumptions about people's behaviour so that it can model economic scenarios through complex mathematics.[10] We won't be doing maths in this book, nor do we need to. People are messy, and they often don't do what you expect them to do. People don't just seek to maximise their profits. Sometimes, they behave altruistically, such as the person who puts a ten-pound note found on the pavement in a charity box rather than in their pocket. Sometimes, they declare war on Ukraine, regardless of the economic consequences that they and their oligarch supporters will face. And more often than not, people are very far away from perfect market information. Yet these assumptions that are at the heart of mainstream economics continue to affect our everyday lives. In this book we draw out these hidden assumptions and demonstrate that they often either do not make sense, or did once make sense but in very different times. After all, our current economic system is now centuries old, the baggage of economic theory has been collecting for a very long time, and it is now weighing us down.[11] This is not, therefore, a history book, but we will have to explore a long time period to understand how mainstream economic ideas affect what we are told we can, and cannot, do.

What is Wrong with Economics?

Outside of mainstream economics, there have been criticisms of economic theory. Robert Skidelsky asks the very question *What's Wrong with Economics?* in the title of his 2021 book aimed at prospective economics students. Likewise, Steve Keen, in his book *The New Economics*, advocates for a complete overhaul of the discipline.[12] Others have taken on the economics discipline in relation to how it has ignored the role of women in the economy; the realities of debt; and the degradation of our environment, to name but three subjects upon which mainstream economics either has little to offer – or upon which what it does offer is downright dangerous.[13] These books that challenge mainstream economics do an excellent job and whilst many of the ideas contained in them inform our thinking, we are not here to reshape the academic discipline of economics.

In this book, we examine the ways in which ideas from mainstream economics have become part of the everyday way in which people generally think about the economic world in which we live. For example, why did people vote for nearly a decade of economic austerity when the absolute last thing an economy in crisis needs is for the government to cut spending? The answer is that the Conservative Party, and in particular, the then Prime Minister, David Cameron, convinced the general public that the national debt was like a personal credit card that had been maxed out and now required repaying.[14] To reinforce the message, the then Chancellor, George Osborne, threatened that failing to lower the UK's national debt would likely lead to a situation where the country's economic woes would be akin to those of Greece. Greece at the time was at the start of a programme of three massive government bailouts by a collective of the European Union, International Monetary Fund, and World Bank (see Chapter Eight).[15] That this did not come to pass in the UK has nothing to do with austerity saving the day and everything to do with the fact that the UK prints its own currency – it simply cannot go bust.[16]

Yet even the mention of the Bank of England being able to print money in order to stimulate an economy under stress inevitably is met by someone invoking interwar Weimar Germany, with apocalyptic images of people wheeling around barrows full of near-worthless money in order to buy even the cheapest and most essential goods. It is true that if money is fixed in value to a commodity, such as gold, or to another currency, such as the dollar, then printing more of it can be quickly inflationary, and can lead to the hyperinflation seen in Weimar Germany. But not since the 1970s have currencies worked like that. Now they float freely, with their value being relative to one another, rather than fixed to a commodity. It is possible, in the right circumstances, i.e. where inflation is already rock bottom and interest rates are near zero, to increase the amount of money in the economy and not cause inflation. Yet the image of the wheelbarrows lingers and, as we will see, is also handy for politicians who prefer austerity over difficult discussions about how to redistribute the wealth in our economy away from the few and towards the many.

We will be looking at the development of economic ideas and how they manifest themselves in our everyday lives because, as the economist Joan Robinson put it, 'the purpose of studying economics is [...] to learn how to avoid being deceived by economists' or worse still, by politicians and social commentators who selectively use economics to validate a particular vision of the social world.[17] This book examines the ideas that underpin our beliefs about how the economy works. We'll see that many of the 'common sense' assumptions about economies and crises are decades, if not centuries old. These assumptions are often based upon subjective value judgements about how people behave. This means that the principles underpinning how society understands and runs its economy owe a lot more to philosophy and politics than to science. And this means that often the limit of what we can achieve is solely the limit of our imagination. Shedding light on the ideas that rule us allows us to understand the challenges facing society at present and to map out the need for future changes to how we think about work and organise the economy. We'll also see how in the contemporary world, politicians have detached specific economic concepts from a broader understanding of how economies work, with such cherry-picking resulting in disastrous economic policies such as austerity.

About the Book

The Ideas That Rule Us focusses largely on the Anglophone world, and in particular the United Kingdom and United States. But many of the ideas seen throughout will be seen to underpin, or to challenge, our thinking on how the economy should be organised not just in the UK and the US but elsewhere, for example in Canada, New Zealand, and Australia. These ideas can be seen within the European Union, particularly when it comes to looking at the banking sector and the financial crisis of 2007–2008. And we will see also how ideas about how the economy should operate were exported, often forcefully, to Latin America from the 1950s onwards.

The book unfolds as follows. In Chapter Two we look at the nineteenth-century underpinnings of economic thinking, in particular about the way in which the individual became prioritised within economics. In this school of thought, everyone is an entrepreneur, trading what they have available. Work is something entered into by a seller of labour (the worker) and a buyer of labour (the employer). In Chapter Three we look at Marx's critique of the classical vision of the worker as entrepreneur and see why Marx saw the employment relationship as exploitative. We will also see that Marx identified aspects of capitalism's operation which made it inherently unstable. In Chapter Four, we look at the causes of unemployment. We see that upon occasion unemployment might be deliberately caused in order to fight inflation and consider what this means in terms of the need to provide a safety net of social security. We will also see that at times, rather than the labour market being an efficient one, there can be periods of chronic unemployment. In Chapter Five we see how John Maynard Keynes proposed to overcome periods of long-term unemployment, kicking off a revolution in economic thinking about the state where, by contrast to the liberals of the nineteenth century, a role for planning the economy was conceded. In Chapter Six, we look at how post-Second World War economic planning oversaw a period of collective economic organisation known as social democracy. During this period, states sought to achieve full employment through economic planning. In Chapter Seven, we see the ways in which those who wanted to hark back to the nineteenth-century small state built upon liberal economic thinking, sowing the seeds of neoliberalism. This is an economic doctrine that believes in a small state but one which has a role to play in the creation of new markets through privatisations and deregulation. In Chapter Eight we see how the ideas of the neoliberals were first spread outside of the countries which gave rise to them, the UK and the US, and how neoliberal economic policies were imposed on Latin America and Greece. In Chapter Nine, we return to the UK and US and see the way in which neoliberal ideas were embedded domestically, rejecting the collective approach to economic organisation which underpinned social democracy and placing the individual economic actor front and centre stage. In Chapter Ten, we see how the process of embedding the individual into a central part of the economy continued in the UK in the New Labour era. We pay particular attention to the gambling industry, an industry which had traditionally been organised on the social democratic principle of protecting people from harm but which was, under New Labour, reconfigured as an industry whose central premise was the individual's right to gamble. In Chapter Eleven, we turn to the 2007–

2008 financial crisis and see how deregulation and the primacy of the market in economic thinking generated a crisis so big that states were required to buy out their banking sectors in order to avoid financial collapse. In Chapter Twelve, we see how the fault for the financial crisis came to be laid at the door of the state and the general public, heralding a period of austerity which made the effects of the crisis worse and which was proved to be totally ineffective. In Chapter Thirteen, we reflect on the academic economics profession in order to demonstrate how it has embedded ideas around the primacy of the individual in the economy into its culture and how this prevents academic economics from engaging meaningfully with discussions about how we should organise our economy to benefit society and people collectively. In the final chapter, Chapter Fourteen, we look at the way in which academic economic thinking has become ineffective at informing political debates on the economy. This makes it extremely difficult for economics to advance our ability to collectively find solutions to societies' problems and makes a case for returning to first principles about what it is we want the economy to do.

But now to the beginning of our story – the ideas of Adam Smith, whose book *The Wealth of Nations* set out much of the basics of modern economics and served as an inspiration to others. In the next chapter, we see that Smith's ideas are still with us and important, as demonstrated by his image being, until recently, reproduced on the reverse of the £20 note. Looking at Smith's work invites us to think about an assumption that many people make, which is that wealth is a reward for effort. From there, in subsequent chapters, we will see that matters are not that simple.

Notes

1 For a critical overview of the basic assumptions of mainstream economics, see Robert Skidelsky, *What's Wrong with Economics?: A Guide for the Perplexed* (New Haven, Yale University Press, 2021) and Rod Hill and Tony Myatt, *The Economics Anti-Textbook: A Critical Thinker's Guide to Microeconomics* (London, Zed Books, 2010).
2 John Maynard Keynes, *The General Theory of Employment, Interest and Money* (London: BN Publishing, 2008), 383.
3 Ibid.
4 For an introduction to Economics by an economist, see Parth Dasgupta, *Economics: A Very Short Introduction* (Oxford, Oxford University Press, 2007). Chapter Four covers supply and demand.

5 For an explanation and critique of the concept of equilibrium, see Skidelsky, *What's Wrong with Economics?*, chapter 4.
6 For a critical assessment of rationality in academic economics see Skidelsky, *What's Wrong with Economics?*, chapter 6.
7 Liam Smith and Celine Klemm, "Even as Behavioural Researchers We Couldn't Resist the Urge to Buy Toilet Paper", *The Guardian*, 5 March 2020.
8 For an overview of what was happening at the time see, Lisa O'Carroll, "What is Causing the UK Crisis in Petrol Supplies?", *The Guardian*, 24 September 2021.
9 UK Parliament, Treasury Select Committee, "Treasury Committee Examines Impact of Russian Energy Sanctions and Effect on Cost of Living", 11 March 2022, https://committees.parliament.uk/committee/158/treasury-com mittee/news/161738/treasury-committee-examines-impact-of-russian-energy-sanctions-and-effect-on-cost-of-living/ (accessed 19 February 2024).
10 See Skidelsky, *What's Wrong with Economics?*, chapter 5.
11 For an overview of the development of economic thought see John Kenneth Galbraith, *The Affluent Society* (London, Penguin, 1998), and, at a thinker by thinker level, Linda Yueh, *The Great Economists: How Their Ideas Can Help us Today* (London, Viking, 2018).
12 Skidelsky, *What's Wrong with Economics?*; Steve Keen, *The New Economics: A Manifesto* (Cambridge, Polity, 2022).
13 For women in the economy see Victoria Bateman, *The Sex Factor: How Women Made the West Rich* (London, Polity, 2019); for debt see Stephanie Kelton, *The Deficit Myth: Modern Monetary Theory and How to Build a Better Economy* (London, John Murray, 2020); for the environment and the economy see Keen, *The New Economics*, chapter 4.
14 Patrick Wintour and Nicholas Watt, "David Cameron to Urge Households to Pay off Debts", *The Guardian*, 5 October 2011.
15 Larry Elliott, "Greek Turmoil Offers George Osborne Justification for his Dictum of Austerity", *The Guardian*, 5 July 2015.
16 Kelton, *The Deficit Myth*, chapter 1 outlines why we should see household and government debt differently.
17 Joan Robinson, *Contributions to Modern Economics* (New York, Academic Press, 1978), 75.

References

Bateman, V. *The Sex Factor: How Women Made the West Rich* (London, Polity, 2019).
Dasgupta, P. *Economics: A Very Short Introduction* (Oxford, Oxford University Press, 2007).
Elliott, L. "Greek Turmoil Offers George Osborne Justification for his Dictum of Austerity", *The Guardian*, 5 July 2015.
Galbraith, J. K. *The Affluent Society* (London, Penguin, 1998).
Hill, R. and Myatt, T. *The Economics Anti-Textbook: A Critical Thinker's Guide to Microeconomics* (London, Zed Books, 2010).

Keen, S. *The New Economics: A Manifesto* (Cambridge, Polity, 2022).

Kelton, S. *The Deficit Myth: Modern Monetary Theory and How to Build a Better Economy* (London, John Murray, 2020).

Keynes, J. M. *The General Theory of Employment, Interest and Money* (London, BN Publishing, 2008).

O'Carroll, L. "What is Causing the UK Crisis in Petrol Supplies?", *The Guardian*, 24 September 2021.

Robinson, J. *Contributions to Modern Economics* (New York, Academic Press, 1978).

Skidelsky, R. *What's Wrong with Economics?: A Guide for the Perplexed* (New Haven, Yale University Press, 2021).

Smith, L. and Klemm, C. "Even as Behavioural Researchers We Couldn't Resist the Urge to Buy Toilet Paper", *The Guardian*, 5 March 2020.

UK Parliament, Treasury Select Committee, "Treasury Committee Examines Impact of Russian Energy Sanctions and Effect on Cost of Living", 11 March 2022, https://committees.parliament.uk/committee/158/treasury-committee/news/161738/treasury-committee-examines-impact-of-russian-energy-sanctions-and-effect-on-cost-of-living/ (accessed 19 February 2024).

Wintour, P. and Watt, N. "David Cameron to Urge Households to Pay Off Debts", *The Guardian*, 5 October 2011.

Yueh, L. *The Great Economists: How Their Ideas Can Help us Today* (London, Viking, 2018).

2

JUST DESERTS

In the 2020 Covid lockdowns, we clapped for NHS workers. But we watch *Casualty* to see the spectacle of trauma, moments when people's lives are changed forever by random events. Medical dramas are not about the actual work of doctors, and whilst we might hail medical professionals as 'heroes', it is because of their ability to 'save' us, not because we appreciate their craft in and of itself. Yet when it comes to entrepreneurs, businesspeople on the frontier of new ventures, it is their craft that is celebrated in popular culture. Decades before Alan Sugar roared, 'You're fired!' at suited business-wannabes on *The Apprentice*, Donald Trump had already (ghost)written a best-selling book entitled *The Art of the Deal*.[1] When it comes to building our society, we celebrate the skill of the entrepreneur. We are fascinated enough by them to analyse them in-depth through how-to guides and reality television – whereas people tend not to want to watch a surgeon remove a diseased gallbladder. The difference between the NHS worker and the entrepreneur is that we assume the NHS worker is paid for by the money created by the entrepreneur. In such a world view, it is not the doctor that saves lives. But, rather, it is the entrepreneur who paid for the hospital and for the doctor's training. Whose company made the ventilators that kept Covid-induced pneumonia patients breathing. The idea that it is entrepreneurs who drive forward progress, innovation, and economic growth in society has been built up over centuries, and in this chapter

DOI: 10.4324/9781003161950-2

we explore how. In doing so, we also get to the heart of the idea that people look to maximise their returns, or in other words, we look at how the idea that 'greed is good' came to be at the centre of mainstream economics.

In 2013, Boris Johnson wrote in the *Daily Telegraph* that the very wealthy are a maligned minority who deserved the then Mayor of London's support as much as the homeless. Proposing 'automatic knighthoods' for 'zillionaires', Johnson was in full flow.[2] Yet with his characteristic bombast, we will see that Johnson was channelling ideas that underpin attitudes about wealth held by many. First, many political economists and moral philosophers, going as far back as Adam Smith, have argued that profits are a reward for risk.[3] In this world view, wealth is justly earned, even the wealth of 'zillionaires'. Second, mainstream economics sees the creation of profits as central to the wealth of everyone. It does so because it assumes that wealth trickles down into the economy as entrepreneurs establish new businesses, expand existing operations, and generate employment and trade for others. These two ideas place entrepreneurs at the centre of society and see their activities as being vital for the common good. By extension, they suggest that society should be focussed around the activities of entrepreneurs, with a small state whose role it is to facilitate and reward the creation of profit. As we will see in Chapter Twelve, for ten years, this was one of the key justifications for austerity. But here, we look at the ideas of the free market, the state, and production which underpinned the thinking of Adam Smith, and also note that they are often used now without reference to Smith's wider points on society.[4]

Smith the Revolutionary

As we will see time and again in this book, with ideas whose influence has lasted a long time, it is important to judge just how valid they are in the current climate, versus the one in which they were written, so that we can properly evaluate the extent to which the ideas should still rule us. Today, we live in a world where Gross Domestic Product (GDP) growth (GDP being the total output of a nation's economy in terms of goods and services) features regularly on the daily news. The idea that economic growth does not occur with each passing year seems outlandish. Yet, in the thousand years prior to the eighteenth century, there had been so little economic growth that what there was had gone largely unnoticed.[5] For the European monarchs of the fifteenth, six-teenth, and seventeenth centuries, the wealth of their nations depended upon encouraging as much wealth as possible into their countries and preventing as much as possible leaving. Britain, for example, passed Navigation Acts – legislation that prevented its colonies trading with anyone but the United Kingdom itself – meaning that, for example, if India wanted to trade with the North American colonies, shipments would have to go through a UK port such as Liverpool or London. And India, which prior to the British industrial revolution had a thriving cotton textile industry, was deliberately deindustrialised by the ruling East India Company. This made India dependent upon exports of raw materials to Britain and open in return to the import of British finished goods such as the very cotton textile goods India had previously made for itself. This was a very strongly regulated economy.

Two broad movements changed this, the 'Dual Revolutions' as the historian Eric Hobsbawm puts it.[6] The first was the French Revolution which, in 1789, brought to an end the absolute power of the French crown to rule over its people. Over the next century or so, limits on the power of monarchs spread throughout Europe. Political constitutions increasingly devolved power from the crown to a universally enfran-chised electorate and its elected representatives. Having written the Declaration of Independence of the United States, Thomas Jefferson found himself in France in its early republican years and assisted in drawing up the Declaration of the Rights of Man and of the Citizen, which similarly underscored the philosophy of the new era in France. Running alongside these political revolutions was an industrial one, originating in Britain, which would greatly increase the economic capa-city and growth of the world economy over the next centuries. And just as the political revolution had, at its heart, a revolutionary zeal to pro-vide liberty and freedom from overbearing government, so too did the industrial revolution. The case for economic liberty was made most notably in *The Wealth of Nations*, first published in 1776, by Adam Smith, a professor of moral philosophy (at its birth, the economics discipline had its home in the humanities) at the University of Glasgow.

Whereas the absolute monarchies of the early modern period had established monopolies to try to safeguard their wealth, Smith realised that this protectionism was counterproductive. Smith argued that eco-nomic growth was indeed possible, and that through free trade there would be an overall increase of wealth for the nation. David Ricardo, whose work we will see below, argued that the benefits of free trade could be global. This stood in stark contrast to the practice of states attempting to close off their economies to imports and maximise their exports – the theory being that in a world where the amount of money was fixed, this was the only way to increase the nation's wealth (an economic perspective which is called mercantilism). Smith's thinking was taken up by Vilfredo Pareto in the second half of the nineteenth century. His concept of what became known as Pareto Improvement argued that free market economies allowed individuals to improve their wealth without diminishing the wealth of others. However, this introduced a problem not foreseen at the time. The continued sharing of prosperity required the economy to continuously grow, something which did not account for limits such as those of the environment.

Whilst the concept of Pareto Improvement was invented after Smith's death, the spirit of it was in Smith's work. For people to gain from economic growth, there needed to be a free market. In other words, not only did the rule of the absolute monarchs need to end for philosophical and moral reasons, as Thomas Paine, author of *The Rights of Man*, argued, but also for economic reasons. Smith conceived that in markets there was present a 'visible hand' and an 'invisible hand'. The visible hand was the actions of the state in markets, generally thought of by Smith and other classical economists as a negative interference. The invisible hand was the market operating without interference, in which the actions of consumers in buying and selling allocate and transfer wealth and goods according to people's willingness to trade at an agreed price between buyer and seller. This, then, was totally incompatible with the old monopolies in which one supplier set a fixed price for goods. It forms the basis of economic thinking today.

The Visible Hand

Smith argued that markets are efficient, and that government intervention disrupts the good operation of markets, creating waste and inefficiency. We saw in Chapter One that this idea is enshrined as one of the basic tenets of economic thinking. To this end, he argued, in the gendered manner of his times, that the state should act as a 'nightwatchman'. To do so, he saw a role for the state in providing laws that regulated society, enforced contracts, and safeguarded private property. After all, there is little point to the accumulation of wealth without recourse to the law to prevent it from being seized from you by others. Likewise, Smith saw the need for law enforcement, and not many years after Smith published *The Wealth of Nations*, the first British police force, indeed the first police force in the world, the Metropolitan Police, was founded. In a similar vein, Smith saw the need for an army to protect from foreign invasion – in other words, against attempts by other states to seize the entrepreneur's private property.

Having established some basic contours for the state, Smith went on to say that it was the state's responsibility to only provide services which it was not in the interests of any one entrepreneur to provide. But Smith did not provide an exhaustive list, and in reality, nor could he have done so in a way that would still be useful today. So, you can imagine that a sewerage network outside your house would get Smith's approval. But what of, as the Labour Party manifesto of 2019 promised, a free national broadband network running to every home? And would, for example, Smith have approved of the National Health Service (probably not) or even primary school education?

Pushed to its limits, anything the state does can be seen as interfering in the market, which to a free-market fundamentalist gives rise to a push for the state to do nothing. For example, in 2022 when the UK government, in an attempt to fight obesity, introduced a law obliging medium- and large-sized restaurants to print on menus the number of calories in their dishes, the Adam Smith Institute issued a blog lampooning the proposal, in the style of 'Yes Minister', under the title, 'Can we Trust Public Health England?'[7] This is pushing Smith's ideas to their limit and beyond. It proceeds from Smith's revolutionary anti-state ideas. But as we have seen, Smith's work was designed to liberate people from autocratic monarchs, not to prevent a modern state from attempting to safeguard the health of the population. We'll return to this tension throughout this book.

Those who are attracted to the small state and free market aspects of Smith's work go by various labels such as libertarians, neoconservatives (in the US, though their beliefs are mixed together with a rich seam of Christian fundamentalism too), and, though more often used as a pejorative by their opponents, neoliberals. In the nineteenth century they went by the name liberal (and later on were referred to by economists as 'classical economists'). But unlike their successors in our time, liberal thinkers like Smith, Ricardo, and John Stuart Mill all had a streak of morality to their economic philosophy. They did not always return to the notion that the market would provide solutions to problems such as poverty or inequality, for example. But increasingly in the twentieth and twenty-first centuries, with the major exception of work inspired by Keynes (see Chapter Five), it was free market fundamentalism that drove economists on. Milton Friedman, Nobel Prize winner in 1977, one of the leading lights at the Chicago School of Economics, and advisor to the Reagan government in the US, went so far as to argue that government should refrain even from regulating the medical profession.[8] Friedman's argument ran that unqualified doctors were likely to be less successful at treating patients, meaning that they would drop out of the market as people avoided them in favour of those doctors who got results. But it's one thing to trust you have perfect market information, or in the age of the internet at least the illusion of it, in order to decide whether or not a Kit Kat is well priced, and quite another when seeking treatment for a life-threatening illness. We'll see more about these free market fundamentalists in Chapters Seven, Eight, and Nine. For now, let us examine the influence of liberal thinking on the operation of the state because this has laid the foundation of debates over what government should, and should not, do in our society.

The Invisible Hand

As we have seen, for Smith the state's role in the economy should be limited. He argued, in fact, that the economy should be guided by the invisible hand of the market (though the phrase 'invisible hand' is only used once in *The Wealth of Nations*). That is to say, the daily transactions of individuals are a better guide for the distribution of society's scarce resources, as the economists put it. This would later influence the work of Friedrich Hayek, as we will see in Chapter Seven, who even thought that this process could be a better democratic alternative to the ballot-box.[9] But for Smith, the free market was essential because it drove innovation.

Smith's economics was what we would now call microeconomics – the economics of the individual or the firm. Within that, Smith saw entrepreneurs as the drivers of innovation. By establishing new business ventures, entrepreneurs tested out the market, finding goods and services that people wanted for the price they were prepared to pay. Those that failed exited the market, but those that succeeded grew the size of the economy through their success. This vision of the economy was based upon the supply of goods. Writing after Smith, a French economist, Jean Baptiste Say, argued that 'supply creates its own demand' (known as Say's law). It was not until Keynes that the issue of demand, who would buy these goods, came to the fore (see Chapter Five).

Smith argued that this wealth generated by entrepreneurs benefitted the whole of society through a 'trickle down' of wealth. As the entrepreneur spent their profits, either on their own consumption or on the expansion of their business interests, the working population benefitted from greater work opportunities. Smith was realistic about this: not everyone benefits in equal measure. In this world view, profits are not an exploitation of workers, as Marx argued (and as we will see in the next chapter), but rather a reward for risk. And the taking of entrepreneurial risk is constantly driving innovation.

The Rational Economic Agent

As we saw in Chapter One, at the heart of economics is what is called the rational economic agent. This mythical person always seeks to maximise their returns. In other words, they always act in their self-interest. Whereas the classical liberals assumed that people moderated their self-interest with some sense of a belonging to a broader society, the hypothetical person used to model economic theory always acts greedily. This leap was necessary the more that economists thought of themselves as scientists who were discovering 'truths' about the operation of the economy. If you want to put people into a mathematical model, you have to have them behaving consistently or the model won't work.[10] And this, then, is a fundamental flaw in mainstream economics – people are messy and don't always behave in one particular way. It is also contrary to Smith's original idea, which related to a self-interested person who nevertheless had a sense of their place in broader society. It also placed individualistic conceptions of the organisation of the economy over collective ones.

It is not just economists who benefit from assuming that people are greedy. That interfering in the market will lead to a collective decrease in wealth has underpinned government policy to taxation. This, then, is why President Trump set about reducing higher-level tax rates for the very wealthy, likewise Liz Truss in her disastrous 44 days as British Prime Minister in 2022. The argument goes that these rates disincentivise additional work by entrepreneurs by making the return on their efforts too small once tax has been taken. Trump and Truss argued that by reducing tax, investment would flow and jobs would be created. Likewise, the New Labour government of 1997–2010 consistently cut corporation tax. By this logic, the pursuit of wealth becomes a virtue. It was a virtue which Boris Johnson praised when the Oxford/AstraZeneca vaccine roll-out was under way during the Covid-19 pandemic in 2021. Johnson was reported as addressing a meeting of fellow Conservatives by declaring, 'The reason we have the vaccine success is because of capitalism, because of greed my friends.'[11] And this is the reason why, above, we saw Boris Johnson arguing for knighthoods for zillionaires. Free market fundamentalists have concluded, at a leap beyond Smith, that, as per Gordon Gekko in the film *Wall Street*, 'greed is good'. Greed, shielding the wealthy from tax, and reducing state regulation, have all become wrapped up in the cloak of 'good economics'. But as we can see, this is not so much good economics, rather it is pushing some principles of liberal economics well past their breaking point for the advantage of particular groups in our economy and society.

An International Free Market and the Division of Labour

The role of the personal pursuit of wealth, and the environment in which it took place, was not just something to be applied within one country. Smith and other liberals saw that specialisation drove innovation. First, they advocated for this in the workplace with consequences for how jobs are viewed, even today. Second, they advocated for specialisation within countries and free trade, a global expression of the small state, to allow for the efficient trade of goods globally. We turn to these two points now.

It was not just realigning the state's involvement in the economy that drove forward the economic explosion of the industrial revolution which Smith was witnessing around him. In *The Wealth of Nations*, Smith focussed on the production of pins (large metal stakes, rather than sewing equipment). Smith observed that in a pin factory set up as a production line, individual operatives, through specialisation, could be part of a volume of production much greater than the same number of individuals each producing a pin from start to finish could achieve. In time, this became most celebrated in the form of Henry Ford's motor vehicle production line. Whereas early car manufacture had focussed on teams of people completing a vehicle together in a workshop, the Ford production line relied on workers simply focussing on one task, for example, repeatedly through the working day attaching wheels to the axles. Smith realised that such work would be so tedious as to pose a mental health risk to the operative. Ford compensated for this through higher wages, though, crucially, in return for workers not being allowed to form a labour organisation. About trade unions, we'll see more in Chapters Six and Nine.

Around the same time as Ford was establishing his car manufacturing business, Frederick Winslow Taylor, an engineer and what we would call today a management consultant, developed the practice of time and motion studies.[12] In this, Taylor insisted that factories be run through scientific measurement of the tasks undertaken in the plant, the refinement of these to produce maximum efficiency, and the repeated following of the protocols subsequently created. If you want to find a striking example of where a time and motion study has produced a workplace layout and working pattern designed around maximum efficiency, go and get a burger in Burger King. Watch the staff, from the moment the order is taken to the moment it is brought to the counter for you. There is a set routine, with the kitchen layout designed to make the operation as quick and efficient as possible. Contrast this with a visit to a restaurant for a sit-down meal. That kind of operation could not possibly produce food at such speed because, even though different chefs have different 'stations', the overall effect aimed at is the high-quality application of the chef's art to a whole serving of varied meals to a table, meals with a freshness that production lines can seldom produce.

Like Ford, Taylor realised that the monotonous jobs his system created would be a mental health hazard for workers. He suggested that these jobs only be offered to those whose 'mental make up was like an ox'.[13] Taylor reduced the worker to a thoughtless beast of burden in pursuit of maximising output and profits. The logic of the market has made many immune to this revelation, the argument being that the market sits outside moral judgements – it simply delivers a good, or service, for a set price. And so, you can justify bad jobs on the basis that the worker accepted an offer to sell their labour for a set price, say, the minimum wage. As we see in the next chapter, Marx pointed out that people have little alternative and this then does raise moral concerns into the operation of the market.

That mechanisation and scientific management create intolerable working conditions was seen in the aftermath of the Covid pandemic of 2020–2022. As restrictions were eased, employers in industries such as fast food and care began to find themselves short of staff. In some cases, there were reasons separate to the work itself that explain this. In the UK, for example, Brexit reduced the ability of people from the European Union to come and work. The UK had been particularly reliant on migrant labour for care homes and fast-food restaurants. But the pattern was also seen elsewhere, leading to what, in the US, was termed the 'great resignation'. That people were disaffected and likely to either leave the labour market or else seek more satisfactory employment elsewhere should not have been a surprise. In 2018, David Graeber outlined an analysis of what he called 'Bullshit Jobs' – jobs that add little value or, worse still, as in the case of much management consultancy, generally just make more work for those who are actually being productive and need no more work to do just to satisfy a box-ticking exercise.[14] In such circumstances, it is little wonder that workers desired to change careers to avoid having to put up with those who occupied these bullshit jobs.

The International Division of Labour

The classical economists saw the need for a division of labour not just within national economies but across them too. David Ricardo argued that it was important for countries to specialise in those industries in which they had a natural advantage (usually due to the existence of particular resources, for example, iron ore, in their territory) and that through the removal of trade barriers people in other countries would benefit from returning goods and services that they were better equipped to produce.[15] Ricardo gave the example of British cotton manufactures, which were cheap and plentiful in the early nineteenth century, and Portuguese port wine. Ricardo argued that it benefitted everyone for Portugal not to make cotton goods and for Britain not to make wine which, if you've ever had English wine, you will know makes perfect sense. Instead, they should concentrate on what they were good at and trade those things with each other, tariff free, so that both countries could enjoy cheaper, higher-quality products. Yet, as we saw above in the case of the deindustrialisation of India, often this exchange was not without power dynamics. Through aggressive free trade policies, rival economies could be made dependent upon larger or growing ones. The problems of supply of goods and labour in the UK post-Brexit are indicative of what happens when a country dislocates itself from networks of international free trade, with prices rising at the same time as productivity has stalled or declined.

Conclusion

Today, Smith's ideas are often associated with the political right. Think tanks such as the Adam Smith Institute advocate for a small-state, low-tax economy. When, in 2022, the Conservative government proposed privatising the television broadcaster Channel 4, the Institute supported this as being consistent with a policy of privatisation designed to reduce the size of the British state, while, at the same time, bringing the supposed benefits of having the broadcaster operate within market forces.[16] Yet when Smith was writing, his desire to reduce the size of the state was designed to empower people who had been subject to the whims of absolute monarchs. His was the era of the Boston Tea Party, where North American merchants protested against taxation imposed by King George III in faraway London, and of the age of the Declaration of Independence. Smith's work was read alongside that of Thomas Paine, who wrote about the 'ridiculous' nature of monarchy, 'It is government through the medium of passions and accidents…it reverses the wholesome order of nature.'[17] So, whilst it is true that Smith advocated many of the ideas that underpin how we view the world today, it is also true to say that they have also been pushed beyond the limits of the context in which they were written, meaning that now they are used to support a particular political agenda in contemporary society and do so in the – borrowed – name of good economics.

The classical liberal economists laid out much of the foundations of how modern economists understand the operation of the economy. But there were differences. The major difference between the classical liberal economists and their successors was that the classicals believed that the value of a good was determined by how much labour had to be applied to the good to produce it, added to the cost of the raw materials to make it. They argued that bread was cheaper than gold because gold required considerably more labour to extract it. This was called the labour theory of value, and as we'll see in the next chapter, Marx threw this theory back in the face of the economists to argue that it was workers and not entrepreneurs who created the wealth of nations. Contemporary economists, following on from the classical tradition and known as neoclassicals, nevertheless made one major shift in the classical theory – they argued that it was not the amount of labour required that determined a good's price but simply the market, through the laws of supply and demand. This was because they saw the value of a good as being different to the price people were willing to pay for it.

Combining the ideas derived from Smith, and the laws of supply and demand, we can now sum up the basic principles behind contemporary economics. Behind the complicated maths that has dominated economics textbooks since the Second World War, economics uses assumptions to build the models by which governments and companies plan for the future. But we might really call these principles beliefs about the human condition, rather than facts. They proceed from the broad church of ideas laid down by the classical liberals. There are four central principles of the economist's faith. First, mainstream economics assumes that people will always seek to maximise their income (this gave rise to the concept of *homo economicus* – the self-interested person). Second, mainstream economics assumes that perpetual growth is possible and desirable. Third, mainstream economics assumes that the production of goods will also produce sales of those goods. Fourth, mainstream economics believes that a global economy, without tariff barriers, allows nations to trade efficiently with each other. By codifying this into models of the world, the real-world ideas of the classical liberals are now supposedly laws of economics, making arguments against them seemingly impossible. These principles are the basis of what is considered contemporary 'good' economics. But are they 'good'? Can we, when faced with literal environmental meltdown, continue pursuing perpetual growth? Is an equitable society possible where the entrepreneur, rather than the worker, is placed at the centre of society? Karl Marx argued not, as we will now see in the next chapter.

Notes

1 Donald Trump and Tony Schwartz, *The Art of the Deal* (London, Arrow Books, 1987).
2 Boris Johnson, "We Should be Humbly Thanking the Super-Rich, not Bashing Them", *Daily Telegraph*, 17 November 2013.
3 For an overview of the ideas of Smith, see Linda Yueh, *The Great Economists: How Their Ideas Can Help us Today* (London, Viking, 2018), chapter

1; Vinay Bharat-Ram, *Evolution of Economic Ideas: Smith to Sen and Beyond* (New Delhi, Oxford University Press, 2017), chapter 1; for the broader liberal tradition in this chapter see John Kenneth Galbraith, *The Affluent Society* (London, Penguin, 1998), chapter 3.

4 It's worth noting that the individualist ideas covered in this chapter and most associated with *The Wealth of Nations* were moderated considerably in his other major work, *The Theory of Moral Sentiments*. Examining *The Theory of Moral Sentiments* is a worthwhile task, but for our purposes we need only focus on the individualism of *The Wealth of Nations* insomuch as it informs mainstream economics today.

5 For a good overview of the coming of Smith's age and an outline of the development of capitalism, see Thomas K. McCraw, *Creating Modern Capitalism: How Entrepreneurs, Companies, and Countries Triumphed in Three Industrial Revolutions* (Cambridge, Massachusetts, Harvard University Press, 1997), chapter 1.

6 Eric Hobsbawm, *The Age of Revolutions: 1789–1848* (London, Abacus, 2005).

7 Tim Ambler, "Can we Trust Public Health England?", *Adam Smith Institute Blog*, 17 May 2022, https://www.adamsmith.org/blog/can-we-trust-public-he alth-england (accessed 20 February 2024).

8 For a good one-stop overview of Friedman's ideas on government policy, see Milton Friedman, *Capitalism and Freedom* (Chicago, Chicago University Press, 1962).

9 Friedrich August Hayek, *The Road to Serfdom* (London, Routledge, 1962).

10 For more on the problems with models in economics, see Robert Skidelsky, *What's Wrong with Economics?: A Primer for the Perplexed* (New Haven, Yale University Press, 2021), chapter 5.

11 Aubrey Allegretti and Jessica Elgot, "Covid: 'Greed' and Capitalism behind Vaccine Success, Johnson Tells MPs", *The Guardian*, 24 March 2021.

12 For Taylor's ideas on scientific management, see Frederick Winslow Taylor, *The Principles of Scientific Management* (London, Dover Publications, 2003).

13 Frederick Winslow Taylor, *The Principles of Scientific Management* (Newark, New Jersey, Norton Library, 1967), 58.

14 David Graeber, *Bullshit Jobs: A Theory* (London, Penguin, 2018).

15 For an overview of Ricardo, see Yueh, *The Great Economists*, chapter 2.

16 Emily Fielder, "Emancipate Channel 4 from State Ownership", *Adam Smith Institute Press Release*, 4 April 2022, https://www.adamsmith.org/news/ema ncipate-channel-4-from-state-ownership (accessed 20 February 2024).

17 Thomas Paine, *The Rights of Man* (London, Everyman, 1966), 168.

References

Allegretti, A. and Elgot, J. "Covid: 'Greed' and Capitalism behind Vaccine Success, Johnson Tells MPs", *The Guardian*, 24 March 2021.

Ambler, T. "Can we Trust Public Health England?", *Adam Smith Institute Blog*, 17 May 2022, https://www.adamsmith.org/blog/can-we-trust-public-health-en gland (accessed 20 February 2024).

Bharat-Ram, V. *Evolution of Economic Ideas: Smith to Sen and Beyond* (New Delhi, Oxford University Press, 2017).

Fielder, E. "Emancipate Channel 4 from State Ownership", *Adam Smith Institute Press Release*, 4 April 2022, https://www.adamsmith.org/news/emancipa te-channel-4-from-state-ownership (accessed 20 February 2024).

Friedman, M. *Capitalism and Freedom* (Chicago, Chicago University Press, 1962).

Galbraith, J. K. *The Affluent Society* (London, Penguin, 1998).

Graeber, D. *Bullshit Jobs: A Theory* (London, Penguin, 2018).

Hayek, F. A. *The Road to Serfdom* (London, Routledge, 1962).

Hobsbawm, E. *The Age of Revolutions: 1789–1848* (London, Abacus, 2005).

Johnson, B. "We Should be Humbly Thanking the Super-Rich, not Bashing Them", *Daily Telegraph*, 17 November 2013.

McCraw, T. K. *Creating Modern Capitalism: How Entrepreneurs, Companies, and Countries Triumphed in Three Industrial Revolutions* (Cambridge, Massachusetts, Harvard University Press, 1997).

Paine, T. *The Rights of Man* (London, Everyman, 1966).

Skidelsky, R. *What's Wrong with Economics?: A Guide for the Perplexed* (New Haven, Yale University Press, 2021).

Taylor, F. W. *The Principles of Scientific Management* (London, Dover Publications, 2003).

Trump, D. and Schwartz, T. *The Art of the Deal* (London, Arrow Books, 1987).

Yueh, L. *The Great Economists: How Their Ideas Can Help us Today* (London, Viking, 2018).

3

TELL ME WHY I DON'T LIKE MONDAYS

During the rail workers' strikes of 2022, Mick Lynch, the General Secretary of the Rail and Maritime Transport Union (RMT), which represents a broad range of transport workers, made a number of media appearances. But rather than his interviewers focusing on the reasons why industrial action was taking place, which included the then cost-of-living crisis (in June 2022, inflation was running at around 10%), proposed longer working hours, and cuts in wages, the discussion revolved around the ideas of Karl Marx, who lived from 1818 to 1883.

On the first day of the rail workers' strikes, ITV's *Good Morning Britain* presenter Richard Madeley asked Lynch, 'Are you, or are you not a Marxist? Because if you are a Marxist, then you're into revolution and into bringing down capitalism.'[1] *Good Morning Britain*'s viewers – more used to a diet of 'Andy Peter's Pancake recipes', showbiz gossip, and the latest from Coronation Street – must have been bemused as to why they were hearing about a political economist who had been dead for nearly 140 years. Later in the day, Sky's Kate Burley asked Lynch if there would be violent confrontations between pickets and agency workers who might be enlisted in an attempt to break the action.[2] Lynch replied that pickets would simply ask such workers not to go into work. Behind him, a few pickets were milling around, hardly looking like a baying mob. That Marx stood in opposition to the capitalist system and saw its end as coming about as the result of a revolution is

DOI: 10.4324/9781003161950-3

true. But for his ideas to be considered so dangerous to our present economic system, they must go beyond simple desires for the future. They must represent a decent critique of the problems of the economy, and society, in which we live.

We look at Marx's ideas in this chapter. First, we look at how Marx understood the process of work and wealth creation, and in doing so drew directly from the ideas of Adam Smith. Second, we look at Marx's ideas about revolution and recognise that these do not undermine his ideas on the operation of our economy.

Marx on Work

In Smith's vision of the economy, workers sell their labour in exchange for goods and services. Our work is treated as a market commodity, just the same as, say, a chocolate bar. In theory, everyone gets out what they put in. But this ignored some tricky questions such as, why some people have more money to deploy in the first place (which created the inequality in wealth that even Smith conceded existed). The answer to this lay in the way in which landownership had been consolidated in the hands of a small number of people during the enclosures movement. This began in the 1600s and steadily consolidated common land into the holdings of landowners, removing its usage by commoners. The locations of many of the hedgerows, dykes, and fences in our countryside today were first laid down as part of that movement. The answer also lay in the slave trade, and in the exploitation of resources in colonies held by Western and Southern European countries. Marx called this primitive accumulation. That the system contained inequalities was rooted in the fact that, from the very start, the playing field had not been level, with some already having more than others.[3]

By the time of the industrial revolution, and right through until today, the economy was broadly divided into two groups: those who could command labour for their business activities; and those who had to sell their labour to earn money to survive. In theory, both groups are made up of entrepreneurs, involved in the sale of goods or services, but in practice, Marx argued that there were real differences between the two which created a broad division of wealth in society. Economists today, based on Smith, see work as a transaction like any other. Two people might agree a price at which they were willing, or unwilling, to pay for a chocolate bar; work is seen in the same way. An entrepreneur offers a job with a set wage; individuals can decide either to accept that wage or, as the economists put it, 'consume more leisure' by not working (we will see that this is important when, in Chapter Four, we look at the causes of unemployment). But Marx saw work differently. For him, it was not a contract of equals, but, rather, an exploitative arrangement.

Mainstream economics assumes that without the need to work to earn a living, individuals will do nothing. Marx argued that, rather than people consuming leisure, more often than not people were constantly having to engage in work in order to survive. With the enclosure of the commons, the idea that one might survive outside of the modern world of work, subsisting from the land, is simply not possible. Because people have to sell their labour to live, Marx called this exploitation. (As an aside, it is worth noting that life before capitalism had hardly been easy and carefree. The image of the country idyll may owe more to the Romantic painters of the nineteenth century than anything else, but the principle still stands.)

For his idea of exploitation, Marx simply took his belief that people were naturally productive and then, using it, repeated back to the classical liberal economists the labour theory of value. In doing so, he agreed with Smith that it was the work that was applied to raw materials (plus the cost of those materials) that gave an item its value. He then pointed out that the worker is forced to return the item or service to the entrepreneur, who sells it for a profit, giving the worker only a small part of that profit – a wage. So, rather than the entrepreneur being the driving force behind the creation of wealth, as Smith argued, Marx pointed out that by Smith's own logic, the entrepreneur simply extracted wealth (or, as Marx called it, surplus value). Marx went on. Instead of the state providing for the rule of law, a police force, and domestic security in order to ensure the prosperity of all participating in a free market economy, Marx argued that the state was there to safeguard the property and wealth of entrepreneurs which were extracted from the workers both at home and overseas (in the latter case through exploitative trade agreements, or through imperial force – or both, as we will see in Chapter Eight).[4]

Another example of Marx simply repeating to classical economics its own ideas, with a modified analysis of what they actually meant, came in his theory of alienation. By alienation, Marx was discussing our relationship with work. He made two major points on this. The first came from the idea that people had to sell their labour to entrepreneurs to earn a living. As we have seen, Marx believed that people are naturally productive. That they are exploited and cannot focus on those things they would prefer to produce, Marx argued, alienated them from work. The second part of alienation related to the type of work people undertake in modern manufacturing processes. We saw in the last chapter Smith's analysis of pin manufacturing and how, after both Marx and Smith's time, Taylor recognised that jobs on production lines reduced people to something akin to a beast of burden (see Chapter Two). Even the language of work in Marx's time disassociated work from people; employees in factories were often referred to as 'hands', as though the rest of the body mattered little. Marx argued that building a system of work that was so loathsome would lead to a system where eventually people would rebel against the conditions in which they found themselves.

To come back to Mick Lynch on daytime TV, the disconcerting thing for economics and for the political establishment is the synergies between the classical tradition and Marx's writings. Smith argued for a small state and some neoliberals have pushed Smith's argument so far that they have become anti-state. Marx agrees, albeit for different reasons. He saw the state as being a bulwark of capitalism and so Marx too wanted to see the disappearance of the state.[5] As we will see soon, though, this was because Marx wanted to replace it with something else. Just as Marx's analysis of the state had potentially worrying parallels with mainstream thought, so too did his analysis of exploitation. If Marx was right, then it is not the entrepreneur who drives innovation and wealth creation but the worker. On that basis, the entrepreneur's rights to profit become non-existent. Little wonder then that Richard Madeley was in such a Marx-induced tizz.

Marx and the Revolution

Marx's ideas on exploitation were based on the same ideas, worryingly for them, as the classical liberals developed. As we saw in the last chapter, later, modern economics rejected the labour theory of value and argued that prices were determined by what the market could bear and not by the amount of labour applied to an object. In doing so, it kept the other ideas that underpinned the classical tradition (such as the laws of supply and demand and the role of the state) and neatly bypassed Marx's ideas on exploitation by cutting from under him the labour theory of value. But, unsurprisingly, the idea that workers create wealth hasn't really gone away, at least for workers. We don't like Mondays because the week will mainly be spent making money for someone else.

Classical economic thinking and the ideas that followed it saw capitalism as being in a steady state. We saw this in Chapter Two – the end to any economic transaction is that the market returns to equilibrium. Thought of like that, our current economic system could continue forever, experiencing shocks only when something external to it interfered, for example, the state setting wages or prices, or trade unions bartering up wages beyond their market level (about which, more in the next chapter). But Marx took a historical view on things, looking back at human history and recognising that economic and political systems had risen, achieved much, and collapsed, only to be replaced by something new. Marx argued that capitalism would collapse and be replaced with something new, in other words that there was nothing unique or final about capitalism.

Just as Marx's arguments about wealth creation and the nature of work could be understood to be inherent to the capitalist system itself – even by the admission of the classical economists – his ideas on revolution were similarly grounded in looking at how the system operated. Marx noticed something which increasingly undermined the economic system. This was its driving mechanism of growth, as per Smith's economics; the entrepreneur's desire to make more money. Marx observed that as businesses failed and the profitable parts of them were bought up by other businesses, a process of concentrating business in the hands of an increasingly small number of very large organisations was unfolding. Amazon's destruction of the high street pays testimony to that. For Marx, capitalism naturally headed in the direction of monopoly, where one firm totally dominated a market (or oligopoly, where a few firms have the market cornered – think Microsoft and Apple). And, by Smith's own admission, the fundamentals of economics rely on the operation of the market.

We can see that over time larger businesses are squeezing smaller ones out of the market. For example, a series of failures of small energy supply companies, such as Robin Hood Energy and People's Energy, totalling 29 between July 2021 and mid-2022, has left energy supply in the UK in the hands of the 'big five' energy suppliers.[6] Despite record increases in energy prices caused by the war in Ukraine, the big five enjoy enormous profits. Only a government-imposed cap on unit prices prevents this oligopoly from indiscriminate price rises. At the core of the companies that enjoy monopoly or oligopoly markets lies a thin seam of super-rich people such as Jeff Bezos (Amazon), Bill Gates (Microsoft), and Mark Zuckerberg (Meta/Facebook). The concentration of wealth amongst this small group of billionaires is astonishing. In the 2019 election, the Labour Party campaigned on the idea that the Conservatives were the party of the '1%'. But in reality, it is not the top 1% in society that is hoarding the most wealth, but the top 0.01% of society that currently controls 11% of the wealth in the global economy.[7] Increasingly, the global economy looks like the end of a game of Monopoly, with only a couple of players going round the board, trying to sweep up the remains from their failed competitors. And when there is only one player left, the game is over.

If the game ended, who would pack the board away? Marx argued that just as the political revolutions of the eighteenth and nineteenth centuries had wrestled power away from monarchs and aristocracies, the fall of capitalism would see workers take power from entrepreneurs. That people would want to do that seemed somewhat self-evident to Marx. By everyone's admission, the system was unequal and the work unpleasant. So, asking Mick Lynch if he is a Marxist is a double-edged sword. On the one hand, it's a question that asks if he accepts Marx's ideas on how capitalism operates. As we have seen, there's little reason not to. On the other hand, media elites would have much to lose in a world which overthrew the current economic set-up. Lynch might represent his self-interested members, but a millionaire TV presenter asking the question 'Are you a Marxist?' was no-less self-interested.

Marx argued that trade unions were useful organisations to teach workers about the flaws in the system and inspire them to seek out change. But he didn't see trade unions as the agents of that change. After all, they spent much of their time bargaining with employers, and bargaining with employers still leaves in place the inequalities that both Smith and Marx identified, albeit diluted. Likewise, Marx saw the coming of 'communism' (the worker-led economic system he wanted to see replace capitalism) as something that had to proceed from the collapse of capitalism. So, whilst countries such as the Soviet Union and People's Republic of China have identified with the politics of Marx, he would not have reciprocated. Marx predicted that the first communist revolutions proper would arise in countries such as Britain, Germany, and the US. This makes sense if we think about his underlying ideas. It was these developed economies where the nature of work and exploitation would become intolerable first. In that sense, there has not yet been a communist country in any sense that Marx meant it because no country has established a communist state in response to the collapse of a capitalist system. And when trade unions take industrial action and the press conjures images of Soviet bread queues, the reality is a long way off Marx's ideas.

Valuing Work

It's worth pausing here and thinking about what constitutes work. The definition of work seemed simple enough for Marx and Smith. It involved applying labour to something and, in the process, increasing its value. But as anyone who, at Christmas, has acted as diplomat to prevent a family argument knows, it's not just waged labour that can be 'hard work'. This is where the idea of social reproduction comes in. Social reproduction is the process by which we make, and remake, ourselves as people. For individuals this might include things like exercise and eating (or better still, eating a healthy diet), but also providing ourselves with shelter and warmth. But across society it might also involve caring for others (such as children, the elderly, or even neighbours), and indeed having children so that humanity itself can be reproduced. It can involve a long list of chores which many of us do, at least at some time in our lives, such as cooking, washing, cleaning the house, and a lot of other things that have taken up the weekend for centuries.

The problem with the housework, of course, is that no one pays you to do it. But it is vitally important. And more broadly speaking, if capitalism is to sustain itself, it needs new markets and fresh workers. Only by reproducing ourselves as a society can the system be sustained. However, the largely unpaid work of sustaining ourselves, as individuals and as a species, has fallen on women. In the UK, the Office for National Statistics estimates that around 60% of unpaid work falls on women.[8] Women undertake 74% of childcare duties in the UK. In a global society that has come to expect this work for free, it is little surprise that globally 80% of paid domestic work is undertaken by women and is poorly remunerated.[9] Mainstream economics does not have much to say about the work done in raising children, caring for the elderly, or indeed simply maintaining ourselves in good health and in relative comfort, in essence because it cannot be quantified in terms of money.

Conclusion

For the classical political economists, profit was a reward for risk. In this world view, people obtain wealth because of hard work and a brave entrepreneurial spirit. In a free market, everyone can trade, be it in goods or their labour, and every transaction is a gain. Yet, if this idea were held by everyone then Monday mornings would not seem so dismal, and low wages would not seem so unfair. As we have seen, the idea that work is inherently exploitative was set out in great detail by Marx. Marx argued that waged labour is exploitative for two reasons. First, it exploits people's natural tendency to be creative. Marx believed that people are naturally creative, but that when they must work for wages to pay for essentials, their creativity is hijacked by an employer. In this sense, Marx argued that waged work 'alienates' us from ourselves. Second, Marx argued that what makes an item have value is the work that is put into it by ordinary workers. For example, it is the carpenter who makes a lump of wood into a chair, yet the entrepreneur who sells the chair takes a profit, despite not having contributed any skill or labour to the chair's production. Marx concluded that freedom could only be achieved in a world where people had control over the work they undertook, and that only a fundamental revolution in how society works will see people fairly rewarded for their work. This conclusion has proved divisive, with some on the political left calling for reform of the existing system and others calling for its complete dismantlement. But no one would remember Marx's ideas if they hadn't proved troubling. In the next chapters, we turn first to the issue of unemployment and the unrest it generates both in society and for economics, before exploring the economics of John Maynard Keynes, who sought to reform economic thinking in part to prevent a situation such as that which Marx predicted coming to pass.

Notes

1 Good Morning Britain, "RMT General Secretary Mick Lynch Quizzed on Whether He's a Marxist amid Biggest Rail Strike", https://www.youtube.com/watch?v=QB4M4ugvaVg (accessed 21 February 2024).

2 Sky News didn't clip that particular piece of coverage, unsurprisingly, but like everything on the internet, it's still out there: "Mick Lynch Explains a Picket Line to Kay Burley", https://www.youtube.com/watch?v=HufDB6QD XTc (accessed 21 February 2024).

3 For a short and reasonably balanced overview of Marx, see Peter Singer, *Marx: A Very Short Introduction* (Oxford, Oxford University Press, 2000); for a sympathetic account see Terry Eagleton, *Why Marx was Right* (New Haven, Yale University Press, 2012).

4 Marx's work in *Das Kapital* is theory-dense, so a good way to get into it is via David Harvey, *A Companion to Marx's Capital: The Complete Edition* (London, Verso, 2018).

5 Eagleton, *Why Marx was Right*, chapter 9 tackles Marx's relationship with the state.

6 "Energy Pricing and the Future of the Energy Market", House of Commons, Business, Energy and Industrial Strategy Committee, 19 July 2022.

7 "The Scale of Economic Inequality in the UK", The Equality Trust, 2022, https://equalitytrust.org.uk/scale-economic-inequality-uk#:~:text=Worldwide%2C%20the%20top%200.01%25%20owned,increase%20in%20wealth%20for%20billionaires.&text=The%20graph%20below%20shows%20how%20wealth%20distribution%20has%20changed%20since,held%20the%20majority%20of%20wealth (accessed 21 February 2024).

8 "Women Shoulder the Responsibility of Unpaid Work", Office for National Statistics, 19 November 2016, https://www.ons.gov.uk/employmentandlabourmarket/peopleinwork/earningsandworkinghours/articles/womenshouldertheresponsibilityofunpaidwork/2016-11-10#:~:text=Women%20carry%20out%20an%20overall,to%20cooking%2C%20childcare%20and%20housework (accessed 21 February 2024).

9 "Changes in the Value and Division of Unpaid Care Work in the UK: 2000 to 2015", Office of National Statistics, 10 November 2016, https://www.ons.gov.uk/economy/nationalaccounts/satelliteaccounts/articles/changesinthevalueanddivisionofunpaidcareworkintheuk/2000to2015#:~:text=In%202015%2C%20mothers%20spent%2C%20on,total%20childcare%20time%20in%202015 (accessed 21 February 2024).

References

"Changes in the Value and Division of Unpaid Care Work in the UK: 2000 to 2015", Office of National Statistics, 10 November 2016, https://www.ons.gov.uk/economy/nationalaccounts/satelliteaccounts/articles/changesinthevalueanddivisionofunpaidcareworkintheuk/2000to2015#:~:text=In%202015%2C%20mothers%20spent%2C%20on,total%20childcare%20time%20in%202015 (accessed 21 February 2024).

"Energy Pricing and the Future of the Energy Market", House of Commons, Business, Energy and Industrial Strategy Committee, 19 July 2022.

"Mick Lynch Explains a Picket Line to Kay Burley", 26 July 2022, https://www.youtube.com/watch?v=HufDB6QDXTc (accessed 21 February 2024).

"RMT General Secretary Mick Lynch Quizzed on Whether He's a Marxist amid Biggest Rail Strike", *Good Morning Britain*, 21 June 2022, https://www.you tube.com/watch?v=QB4M4ugvaVg (accessed 21 February 2024).

"The Scale of Economic Inequality in the UK", The Equality Trust, 2022, http s://equalitytrust.org.uk/scale-economic-inequality-uk#:~:text=Worldwide% 2C%20the%20top%200.01%25%20owned,increase%20in%20wealth%20for %20billionaires.&text=The%20graph%20below%20shows%20how%20wea lth%20distribution%20has%20changed%20since,held%20the%20majority% 20of%20wealth (accessed 21 February 2024).

"Women Shoulder the Responsibility of Unpaid Work", Office for National Statistics, 19 November 2016, https://www.ons.gov.uk/employmentandla bourmarket/peopleinwork/earningsandworkinghours/articles/womenshoulder theresponsibilityofunpaidwork/2016-11-10#:~:text=Women%20carry%20out %20an%20overall,to%20cooking%2C%20childcare%20and%20housework (accessed 21 February 2024).

Eagleton, T. *Why Marx was Right* (New Haven, Yale University Press, 2012).

Harvey, D. *A Companion to Marx's Capital: The Complete Edition* (London, Verso, 2018).

Singer, P. *Marx: A Very Short Introduction* (Oxford, Oxford University Press, 2000).

4

UNEMPLOYMENT

We saw in Chapters One and Two that a central idea in economic thinking is that markets are efficient. Two people engage in an exchange, at a price that they can both agree, the market clears, and the cycle begins again. By this logic, the current economic system could go on forever, tending as it does, in theory, back to equilibrium. In Chapter Three, we saw that Marx disagreed with this, and argued that there were a number of inbuilt problems in the economic system. If Marx were wrong about this, no one would be asking trade union leaders whether or not they are a Marxist on daytime television, well over a hundred years since Marx's death. That there are problems inherent in the economy is what has kept Marx's ideas in people's minds. And whilst his ideas have not necessarily 'ruled' the average person in the UK, the attempts by politicians and economists to work out ways in which Marx's ideas on revolution will not come about certainly have.

One of the major problems which economics struggles to satisfactorily explain, or solve, is unemployment. In theory, someone who wishes to sell their labour should be able to find a price at which they can do so, creating an equilibrium and clearing the market for labour. But the problem of unemployment has not gone away. Indeed, the scale of the problem has at times been vast, leading to desperate action. Protest marches against mass unemployment litter history, some better remembered than others. In 1905, 500 unemployed workers from Leicester

DOI: 10.4324/9781003161950-4

marched to London in protest of high unemployment in their city. Today, a plaque in Leicester market square remains to commemorate the event. Channelling Marx's ideas, the plaque is inscribed with, 'The profits of the earth are for all to share.' More famously, in 1936, during the middle of the Great Depression (about which, more in the next chapter), a group of 200 workers marched from Jarrow, in the North East of England, to London to present a petition to Parliament demanding that work be provided in the hard-hit industrial town. Whilst unsuccessful, the march has become a symbol of the need for social reform that allows people to work and avoid poverty.

The long history of unemployment marches runs right up to the present. In 2012, in Spain, two separate marches converged on Madrid, one coming from Barcelona and the other from Andalucía. At the time, Spain was suffering from massive unemployment, specifically high youth unemployment, which came in the wake of the financial crisis of 2007–2008 (of which, more in Chapter Eleven).[1] Remember, Smith's economics was the economics of supply, and of the individual and the firm – microeconomics. Why was the supply of labour not being taken up? How had Say's law – that supply creates its own demand – failed? Four main ideas prevail in the mainstream. We investigate them here, only to find that they are not always satisfactory, leading us in the next chapter to the writing of John Maynard Keynes. Keynes saw the problems inherent in classical economics. However, he was no Marxist. Keynes set himself the job of saving capitalism from itself by revolutionising economic theory, not society.

Frictional Unemployment

As we will now see, mainstream economics explanations for unemployment put the blame for it on individuals and argue against collective action to resolve it. The first of the four mainstream explanations for unemployment is frictional unemployment. People move from job to job. There are certain short-term barriers that prevent them from immediately starting their new employment. In other cases, people may choose to finish one employment before having another in order to pivot their career from one industry to another, requiring a period of research about the new industry and perhaps learning new skills. This is called frictional unemployment. We might, arguably, count under this banner those who have been part of the 'great resignation' and those who exit the labour market to undertake caring responsibilities. (Though, the former might be classed as 'consuming more leisure', see below, and the latter as simply being no longer part of the formal economy.) In many ways, frictional unemployment isn't much to worry about and might even be a sign of a healthy economy, bursting with opportunities and optimism for future aspirations. But it does raise a couple of interesting issues. First of all, we see that the market isn't able to automatically and immediately revert back to equilibrium. Sometimes people have other things to do than follow the theory of the market around. If it is true that in the labour market the market does not adjust instantly, it can be true of others. We'll see in Chapter Thirteen that the idea that markets automatically adjust to equilibrium only works in theory. Second, it does suggest that at any one point in time there might be a 'natural' rate of unemployment that cannot be tackled, not least of all because, in the case of most frictional unemployment, there is no obvious need to tackle it. As we will see in later chapters, this idea has more weight to it and stood opposed to the idea that economies could provide employment to all who want it.

Structural Unemployment

Structural unemployment is where resources are focussed in the wrong place, creating unemployment. A tour of the former mining villages of West Yorkshire gives a pretty stark demonstration of structural unemployment. There, between 1981 and 2004, only 83% of coal-related jobs were replaced after the governments of Margaret Thatcher and John Major undertook a programme of pit closures that all but ended the UK mining industry.[2] The skills of former miners struggled to find use in the deindustrialised economy. More recently, the lockdowns that were instituted during the Covid-19 pandemic created structural unemployment by changing the nature of city centres. Previously busy areas with shops dedicated to providing workers with food, drink, and other items found, and continue to find, themselves with no customers as people worked from home, and in many cases still do. Whether or not the high street can recover against the massive shift to online retail and work remains to be seen.

As we have seen, in theory the problem should solve itself. People unable to command a price for their labour in one area should, through market forces, relocate to another area where they can. There are some market-based reasons as to why this might not happen. For example, unemployment in the North of England is hard to solve via a policy of job creation in London due to the higher cost of living in the South East. But more than this, the reality of the situation is that people's cultural, spiritual, and familial ties with an area often transcend market forces. Often, breaking those ties occurs only in a cataclysmic event such as the Irish Potato Famine of 1845–1849, when over one million people left Ireland (by the end of the famine around one-quarter of the population was dead or had emigrated). The general unwillingness to relocate, except in the most extreme of circumstances, can create a ready population of discontented people. In 2016, in the US, the so-called 'rust belt' states were suffering large-scale unemployment due to relocations of heavy industry, in particular car manufacture, elsewhere in the US and overseas. The people in these states proved especially susceptible to Donald Trump's 2016 election campaign in which he promised to return jobs to these areas. In the process, he won himself some key swing states and the election.[3] This was a reminder that people do not necessarily look to progressive answers to hard times and may turn to reactionary ideas instead. The promised jobs were, of course, a pipedream.

Classical Unemployment

If we put aside frictional and structural unemployment, then we are left with explanations that draw upon the classical equilibrium model being disturbed by some outside force (hence classical unemployment). As we have seen, in the classical model, the buyer and seller of labour agree a price, the market clears, and the process begins again. But in classical unemployment, some person or organisation acts to raise the price of labour above what the market will bear. For example, a highly union-ised workforce would be in a position to demand higher wages. But there could come a point at which the entrepreneur would expect either such a low return, or none at all, given the cost of labour, that they decided not to continue production and, rather, to relocate or close. In turn, unemployment would be caused.

The problem of trade unions raising prices through collective action was realised early on in the development of capitalism. In an attempt to prevent this, though more for the benefit of employers than the workers, trade unions in early-nineteenth-century Britain were outlawed. They were legalised under severe restrictions in 1825 but attempts to restrict trade union activity continued. In 1834, a group of six farm labourers in Tolpuddle formed a friendly society to protest against declining agricultural workers' wages. They were subsequently arrested under an obscure act which legislated against the swearing of secret oaths. In an attempt to frighten others away from forming labour organisations, the judge in the case sentenced the six men to transportation to Australia. The penalty was so excessively severe that the six became known as the Tolpuddle Martyrs, and two years later, after considerable popular protest, they were pardoned.

Later acts opened up the legislation further. But as late as 1901, a legal precedent set in the case of the Taff Vale Railway company versus the Amalgamated Society of Railway Servants effectively outlawed strike action when it found that trade unions could be held liable in civil proceedings for restraint of trade through industrial action. Though repealed in 1906, this case was the beginning of a significant change in British politics – it forced trade unions to seek representation in Parliament, forcing the creation of the Labour Party. The party would first form minority governments in 1924 and 1929 and then, in 1945, a majority government that founded the British welfare state. The idea that trade unions should be restrained, or even banned, in order to protect the free market in labour is a powerful one. Not just for those who genuinely believe it, but also for those who worry trade unions allow for collective action that might threaten profits or indeed perhaps capitalism itself.

In addition to the idea that the 'natural' rate of the price of labour might be distorted by trade unions, a similar school of thought exists in relation to state-imposed minimum wages. Here, the visible hand of the state disturbs the market by setting minimum prices that might be above the equilibrium level. This is one of the reasons why governments have often resisted attempts to introduce one. In the UK, it was only in 1998 that a minimum wage was introduced amid a heated debate, one side of which predicted – or scaremongered – that mass unemployment would be the result. In fact, the lowest unemployment in over 20 years came after the introduction of the minimum wage. It's worth noting that not all mainstream economists think negatively about minimum wages today. We'll see below that issues of demand have to be taken into account. But to foreshadow a little bit, the answer to the question 'how will I pay a £15 minimum wage?' is 'through customers spending their £15 minimum wage'.

The debate has not gone away, nor has it always been pleasant. In 2011, a Conservative MP, Philip Davies, argued in the House of Commons that the minimum wage was causing unemployment amongst people with disabilities because it forced the price of labour by people with disabilities above the equilibrium value. Addressing the House, Davies argued, 'for some people the national minimum wage may be more of a hindrance than a help' on the basis that 'people with a learning disability clearly, by definition, cannot be as productive in their work as somebody who has not got a disability of that nature'. He proposed suspending the national minimum wage for people with cognitive or intellectual impairments. Criticism of his position was dismissed by Davies as 'left-wing hysteria'.[4]

Whilst we might consider Davies's position an ableist or discriminatory one, the logic of the position is based on the idea in classical economics that the state distorts the market in counterproductive ways. It demonstrates how 'good' economics, seen as neutral, can be used to absolve legislators of the need to consider issues of morality.

Voluntary Unemployment

Behind the concept of classical unemployment is, essentially, a protest that markets function well in theory and that if they're not functioning well in practice, someone, or some organisation, is mucking things up. Whereas classical unemployment occurs when employers don't want to pay the price at which work is offered, voluntary unemployment is the opposite, where workers don't take up the price offered for their work. Voluntary unemployment takes forward the sentiment that something is interfering in the market when looking for reasons as to why people do not work at the market rate.

Some of the reasons why people might be declining employment might relate to the welfare or tax systems. For example, in the 1970s in the UK, the higher marginal tax band was 83% on earned income.[5] The argument runs that at these levels, there is little incentive to earn above the threshold for the highest rate given the smaller returns. Certainly, this was the era of pop stars and actors, such as Michael Caine, fleeing to the US to avoid the UK tax regime.

At the other end of the spectrum, the political right has often followed the logic that welfare payments might make not working attractive to some. These days, you often hear right-wing politicians stating that benefits are 'too generous'. But the suspicion that people will malinger on benefits has a long history. After all, the introduction of workhouses was based on the belief that people would prefer poor relief to employment, so unemployment had to be made intolerable through harsh labour. Frighteningly, the last workhouses were only closed in 1948 and the spirit of the workhouse lingers on. The coalition government from 2010 and Conservative governments from 2015 have introduced a number of 'workfare' schemes where benefits are paid only to those who accept unwaged work placements. The schemes have not been uncontentious. Tesco, Poundland, and Argos used labour obtained from the schemes, suffering significant public outcry at companies making profits from work paid for by government benefits.[6] The idea that social security interferes with the market, and appeals to people's laziness, is a recurrent one, and we will return to it in later chapters.

Unemployment and Inflation

We noted above that in classical unemployment, one cause of unemployment could be that the state has interfered with the market in some fashion, such as by setting a minimum wage. Another way this could happen is through the incorrect setting of interest rates. We'll come back to how this works soon, but first let us consider interest rates. Interest rates have two important functions in the economy. The first is that they indicate the return on savings that individuals or businesses will get from their deposits with banks. The second is that they determine how much individuals or businesses pay to borrow money from banks (and how much banks pay to borrow money from their central bank, in the UK case the Bank of England). This is why, when interest rates go up, those with savings (usually older people) are pleased, and why those with mortgages (usually younger people) pay out more.

In the UK, the Bank of England, following a mandate from the government, sets what is called the 'bank rate'. This is the rate at which banks pay to borrow money from the Bank of England. Banks themselves set their own interest rates with regard to the bank rate, so if the bank rate goes up, then so will the interest rates that you and I will be offered if taking out a mortgage or credit card. Likewise, if the bank rate comes down, so too does the cost of borrowing.

Raising or lowering the bank rate can encourage either saving (through a high rate that makes keeping money in the bank attractive) or spending (through a low rate that makes saving unattractive and loans cheap). In this way, the Bank of England can influence people's spending, and through that, the rate of inflation in the economy. This is called monetary policy. Here's how it works. The idea is that through adjusting the base rate, the Bank of England can keep inflation at around a steady 2%. This is because it is usually assumed that inflation and employment are in opposition to each other. If plenty of people are unemployed, then the amount of purchasing power (demand) in the economy will be low and so too, therefore, will inflation. However, if there is nearly full employment in an economy demand will be high, driving up inflation because there will be more money chasing the same amount, or fewer, goods and services. But it's also true that the Bank of England plucked the exact figure of 2% out of thin air so the principles are more important than the actual figure.

For the past 30 years or so, governments and central banks have attempted to control unemployment and inflation by changing the costs of spending and the benefits of saving. When inflation is low, or negative, indicating economic stagnation or a recession, the central bank can lower interest rates. This makes the incentives to save much weaker and should divert people's spare cash into investments which, in turn, should promote growth and increase employment. (Remember from previous chapters, economics places the entrepreneur at the heart of wealth creation, so promoting their activities is entirely in keeping with the ideas of the classical liberals which we saw in Chapter Two.) The opposite is also true: if inflation is high, central banks can raise interest rates, which prompts people to pull out of investments and move their money into savings. But it also has another effect: as the economy slows down, unemployment rises. In this sense, there is a deliberate attempt to create unemployment in order to reduce demand and, therefore, inflation.

Is inflation a good enough reason to deliberately make people unemployed? Inflation can most certainly be an extraordinary problem. Low inflation signals an economy in trouble and is usually accompanied by unemployment. In Japan, poor economic growth was considered such a problem that the Bank of Japan, between 2016 and 2024, imposed a negative bank rate. In other words, savers were actually charged for saving in an attempt to boost investment. Whilst low interest rates can be good for businesses, as they allow for cheaper borrowing for expansion or upgrading of current facilities, they do reduce the income of those who rely on savings, such as pensioners. But whilst high interest rates would benefit savers, high inflation whittles down the spending power of those in work, disincentivises investment by businesses, and raises the level of unemployment.

The stakes are clearly high when it comes to setting interest rates. They will inevitably hurt some section of society before they manage to return inflation to the 2% target. But determining whether or not to tackle inflation using interest rates in the first place is difficult. For a start, the effects on inflation of altering interest rates take some time to filter through. For example, if interest rates are lowered, not everyone can switch from savings to investments instantly. And some savers, such as pensioners, are likely to wait a while anyway; given that savings are their principal source of income, they are likely to be wary about moving quickly to investments. This means that altering interest rates in the case of short-lived inflation would be meaningless and create more harm than good. Worse still, in the longer term, altering interest rates might not work at all. Japan's negative interest rate has not had the desired effect. And there is only so low that you can go. In the UK case, the Bank of England decided that 0.1% was the lowest rate it could practically set, but growth has still been sluggish with Covid and the Russia–Ukraine war both knocking the economy into recession.

The lowest rate at which the bank rate can be set is known as the 'zero lower bound' because, in theory, zero is the lowest you can go on interest rates. In reality, the lower bound might be either side of zero. But once there, if growth is not forthcoming, adjusting interest rates is no longer a viable tactic for improving growth. The other matter to consider is the cause of the inflation. Above, we have looked principally at inflation that is being driven by full employment and high demand. In other words, more money chasing the same amount of, or fewer, goods. However, it could be, as occurred in the global economy after the Russian invasion of Ukraine, that inflation is being driven by a decrease in supply, i.e. the same money chasing even less gas and oil (or whatever the product might be). Of course, inflation can happen on individual items. A failed wheat harvest will see the price of bread and beer increase. But if it is happening over a number of different goods (for example, as a result of increased costs caused by Brexit) or on some key items (oil and gas are used in every part of production, from energy production to transport to the consumer), then inflation will be seen across an economy.

Conclusion

Despite Marx's belief that humans are naturally productive, and the belief of mainstream economics which holds that individuals are self-interested, seeking always to maximise their returns, there runs through the welfare system a core belief that people are work-shy. We have looked at the reasons for unemployment as a means to explain this contradiction. In classical economics, four things explained involuntary unemployment. First, someone might be unemployed for a very short period whilst moving between jobs (known as frictional unemployment). Second, unemployment might be caused by a lack of skills or by skills and labour being located in the wrong parts of the economy, known as structural unemployment. Third, people might be unemployed because the market for labour had somehow been distorted so that people wanted more money for their labour than employers were willing to pay, i.e. classical unemployment. In the absence of these three types of unemployment, the only explanation left is that people are choosing to be unemployed. This belief is reconciled to the self-interested economic actor idea by reckoning that when people are voluntarily unemployed, they are 'consuming' leisure. And if you believe that, then workhouses for the 'feckless' poor make some kind of sense, likewise the more contemporary 'workfare'. However, we have seen that in order to control inflation, unemployment might be deliberately created. As we will see in Chapter Five, the classical explanation misses out an important consideration, namely, the idea that there might simply not be enough work to go around.

Notes

1 Stephen Burgen and Philip Inman, "Spain Faces Crisis 'of Huge Proportions' over Unemployment and Banks", *The Guardian*, 27 April 2012.
2 Christina Beatty, Stephen Fothergill, and Ryan Powell, "Twenty Years on: Has the Economy of the UK Coalfields Recovered?", *Environment and Planning A* 39, no. 7, 2007: 1654–1675.
3 Michael McQuarrie, "Trump and the Revolt of the Rust Belt", LSE Blog, 11 November 2016, https://blogs.lse.ac.uk/usappblog/2016/11/11/23174/ (accessed 21 February 2024).
4 Allegra Stratton, "Tory MP Philip Davies: Disabled People Could Work for Less Pay", *The Guardian*, 17 June 2011.
5 Alan Manning, "Top Rate of Income Tax" (London, London School of Economics, Centre for Economic Performance, 2015), https://cep.lse.ac.uk/pubs/download/ea029.pdf (accessed 21 February 2024).

6 Shiv Malik, "Poundland Case: A Story we Couldn't Have Told Without Our Readers", *The Guardian*, 30 October 2013.

References

Beatty, C., Fothergill, S., and Powell, R. "Twenty Years on: Has the Economy of the UK Coalfields Recovered?", *Environment and Planning A* 39, no. 7, 2007: 1654–1675.

Burgen, S. and Inman, P. "Spain Faces Crisis 'of Huge Proportions' over Unemployment and Banks", *The Guardian*, 27 April 2012.

Malik, S. "Poundland Case: A Story we Couldn't Have Told Without Our Readers", *The Guardian*, 30 October 2013.

Manning, A. "Top Rate of Income Tax" (London, London School of Economics, Centre for Economic Performance, 2015), https://cep.lse.ac.uk/pubs/download/ea029.pdf (accessed 21 February 2024).

McQuarrie, M. "Trump and the Revolt of the Rust Belt", *LSE Blog*, 11 November 2016, https://blogs.lse.ac.uk/usappblog/2016/11/11/23174/ (accessed 21 February 2024).

Stratton, A. "Tory MP Philip Davies: Disabled People Could Work for Less Pay", *The Guardian*, 17 June 2011.

5

THE GENERAL THEORY

In Chapter Four, we saw that, in mainstream economics, sustained high unemployment should not exist. Markets are assumed to be efficient; they move towards equilibrium, and they clear (which is to say that the price of a good or service will always find a level at which it will be sold). Some temporary unemployment might exist if people are moving between jobs (frictional unemployment). If people lack particular skills or are in the wrong location, they may be unemployed until they reskill and/or relocate to an area where they can find employment (structural unemployment). Causes of longer-term unemployment could be that people are voluntarily unemployed, either because they are leisured or because they can subsist on welfare payments. In other cases, the visible hand might be distorting the market by using labour market advantages to force wages above the market price (classical unemployment). Broadly speaking, causes of unemployment were deemed to be either short-lived, or the fault of external forces that could be 'corrected', generally by somebody somewhere reverting to doing nothing about the problem.

The ideas behind these types of unemployment fit with the micro-origins of mainstream economics, which focussed on the individual or the firm. Because this view saw entrepreneurs as the driving force in an economy, it focussed on the supply of goods and services. As we have seen, this is summed up in Say's law as, 'Supply creates its own

DOI: 10.4324/9781003161950-5

demand.' Or, as *Wayne's World* put it, 'If you book them, they will come.' The problem was that unemployment reoccurred and was sometimes persistent throughout the nineteenth century and into the twentieth. In 1929, the Wall Street crash ushered in the Great Depression, a period of extended unemployment around the world, much as the financial crisis of 2007–2008 ushered in what has been dubbed the Great Recession.[1]

During the 1930s in the UK, the number of unemployed reached around three million people, and the problem continued until the outbreak of the Second World War in 1939. This was the era of some of the most iconic and harrowing pieces of literature about poverty and its effect on communities such as Orwell's *The Road to Wigan Pier*, and Arthur Greenwood's *Love on the Dole*.[2] Had Marx's prediction come to pass? Was the machinery of economics now grinding to a halt?

Into this conundrum came John Maynard Keynes (known as Maynard Keynes to distinguish him from his economist father John Keynes). Keynes was a political economist at the University of Cambridge. Unlike Marx, he was no revolutionary, but, like Marx, he was a visionary. Keynes noticed that, at times, high unemployment was persistent but that it could not be explained by the four concepts laid out by mainstream economics. Long-term unemployment was too prolonged to be frictional or structural. As to classical or voluntary unemployment, welfare payments were very modest in the interwar period. And in a high unemployment economy trade union power was weakened, not strengthened.

Keynes realised that the problem was one of demand – with insufficient demand for goods and services in an economy, firms would be disinclined to take on workers. But if people have no work, then they cannot buy goods and services. After the more recent recessions, and the austerity that followed the financial crisis of 2007–2008, Keynes' idea – that if people have no money to spend, the economy will not recover – seems obvious to us. But a revolution was needed in economic ideas in order for this idea to be deemed worthy of action by the state and other organisations and interest groups. Keynes was well placed to lead this change of ideas. He had access to the political establishment, having served in the Treasury during the First World War; he was a respected academic writer; and he was an accomplished journalistic writer and public speaker.[3]

In this chapter, we look at the ideas that Keynes came up with to tackle the economic recession that lingered throughout the 1930s. First, we look at the problems with the mainstream model. Second, we see how Keynes proposed to solve them by looking not at supply, but at demand. This was more than simply looking at the other side of the process of exchanging goods and services. Keynes directed the focus of economic thought away from the individual or the firm to the national economy as a whole, giving rise to macro-economics.

Problems with the Mainstream Models of Unemployment

Keynes first set about diagnosing the problems that supply and demand encountered when applied to unemployment by mainstream economics. As we saw in Chapter Four, in the classical model, the price at which employers are willing to pay for work and the price at which workers will sell their labour should be constantly balancing out to equilibrium. In this way, the market's efficiency is maintained, avoiding unemployment. However, Keynes realised that in the real-world market for labour, wages did not adjust as quickly as was needed for the model to work. He argued that, rather than being quick and fluid, the price of labour was 'sticky', more like a viscous glue. This is hardly surprising; after all, if someone is being paid a particular wage one week and then paid 10% less for the same amount of work the next, they are not likely to readily accept it. And if a workplace is highly unionised, the ability to resist cuts is further enhanced.

Because wages are sticky, the vision of economics – that prices in labour will adjust down quickly in a recession – does not come about. Because of this, there is no supply of cheap labour which entrepreneurs can call upon to help them turn out products at lower prices, in the hope of stimulating demand. Of course, one answer to this problem would be for firms to lower their prices. But here too Keynes argued that prices in general are also 'sticky' (more of this in Chapter Thirteen).

There may be some sensible reasons for firms not to lower their prices; for example, adjusting prices might mean costs are incurred in altering advertising materials or trade catalogues. Or firms might worry that decreasing the price of a good or service might undermine the brand, making it seem substandard. Firms might also be 'locked in' to a deal to offer a product for a certain price for a certain amount of time. But, just like people as explored in earlier chapters, firms often don't act as rational economic agents. A firm might resist lowering prices simply because they perceive that the risk of the product going unsold is lower than the risk of a loss of return by lowering its price. With sticky wages and prices clogging up the market model of economics, it became clear to Keynes that any change in terms of lowered demand, investment, or government expenditure would have an effect on the number of goods and services sold in an economy.

Typically, governments up to the Second World War and since the 1980s have not tried to affect demand in a recession. Instead, governments have used interest rates to encourage investment. By making the cost of borrowing low, and the returns on savings similarly low, the idea is to encourage firms to invest and increase output. As we saw in Chapter Four, at that point the cost of borrowing is as cheap as it can be, and there is little reason to save given the poor interest returns on holding cash. Between 2016 and 2024, Japan even adopted a negative interest rate, where people lost money by saving it. Yet, despite these efforts, Japan's economy remained in a poor state. Keynes described people's attitudes as 'animal spirits', where people act not out of rational understanding of the maths involved in investments, but rather a collective 'feel' of whether or not investment would be a good idea. But if confidence in the market is low, there can come a point where businesses refuse to invest, no matter how cheap it might be to raise the finance to do so. This brings us back to Keynes' main point – that if business will not invest in a prolonged downturn, the only organisation that can is government.

Insufficient Demand

Whilst classical economics believes that supply creates its own demand, Keynes foresaw situations in which this was not true. In this way, Keynes examined the problem of unsold goods in a firm, industry, or national economy. Keynes argued that, in a recession, people are unlikely to want to spend at the same rate as in good times. This is true both for consumers and for firms. This argument has been underscored by the cost-of-living crisis that began in the UK in early 2022. The crisis was a result of the rising cost of energy, caused by the war in Ukraine, and the rising cost of food imports, caused by Brexit. For Keynes, it was lower aggregate demand that causes an economy to sink into recession. Or put the other way, it is the sum total of government, business, and household spending that is the main driving force in an economy.

Recessions are, of course, messy and worrisome. Real wages fall, and unemployment increases. Many who can increase their savings do so in order to buffer themselves against unforeseen economic difficulties down the road. Keynes called this 'the paradox of thrift'. When people save during a recession, they reduce the amount of buying power – demand – in the market. The paradox of thrift was demonstrated quite starkly in 2010, by David Cameron's election campaign and the Conservative Party's subsequent government coalition with the Liberal Democrats. Cameron ran using the idea that the financial crisis of 2007–2008 had been caused by excessive spending by the then Labour government (it was not, as we will see in Chapter Twelve). Cameron often talked about 'the nation's credit card', and how it needed to be paid off after being maxed out.[4] We will see in a bit why this wasn't the case. But, over the period from the election to late 2011, Cameron provoked the paradox of thrift by his credit card analogy. Individuals took Cameron's message to heart and began paying off personal credit card debt. The economy started to slow perilously; the Treasury became worried that the recession was going to worsen. Cameron had to hastily rewrite his 2011 Conservative Party Conference speech to make it clear that he was not instructing households to pay off credit card debt. And this was exactly Keynes' point: in a recession, reduced demand makes the problem even worse.

Government Spending and the Multiplier Effect

Keynes was familiar with the economic thinking that was popular in the UK Treasury in the interwar period, after his own spell there during the First World War. In sharp contrast to his own thinking, the 'Treasury View' was that the state should adopt economic ideas derived from classical economics such as a small state, low taxation, and sparse regulation of business. In a recession, the Treasury's default position was to trim expenditure in line with decreased tax income, resulting in cuts to public services. The idea was that by controlling government spending, businesses would have more money to invest. And by not actively investing in the economy, there would be no danger of government 'crowding out' business investment (where businesses don't invest because they expect the government to do it for them). In this view of national economic management, the economy would recover from recession in the long run by the efforts of businesses and the operation of the free market. But Keynes made an important counterpoint to this:

'in the long-run we are all dead.' He went on, 'Economists set themselves too easy, too useless a task if in tempestuous seasons they can only tell us that when the storm is long past the ocean is flat again.'[5] Keynes' idea was this: that when economies are caught in the paradox of thrift, only the government can get the economy going again by investing when business will not.

Proposals for government spending are often greeted by the right-wing press with calls as to who will pay for the cost of borrowing. Yet Keynes has an answer for this. The projects which he proposed for government investment with the aim of stimulating demand were designed to be ultimately self-financing. Keynes proposed that projects should be reasonably shovel-ready. That is to say, in a recession there is no point in trying to stimulate demand through a project that won't get off the ground for 20 years, if at all (hence why the now truncated HS2 high speed rail line has done nothing to boost the economy despite the scale of the money involved). Then Keynes proposed that the projects to be invested in should leave a benefit or increase capacity in some way. In Keynes' day, such projects might have included roads or hydro-electric dams (in the 1930s, Keynes' ideas were more popular in the US and the Hoover hydroelectric dam owes much to Keynes' championing of infrastructure projects). A more contemporary initiative might be the rolling out of high-speed fibre-optic cabling countrywide.

Because government investment would leave behind useful infrastructure, it would be able to boost economic growth in the future which itself would generate higher tax returns to pay back the initial money paid out for the project. Better still, moving people off unemployment benefit and into jobs would cut costs to the government. But it is worth noting that Keynes' ideas were meant to be applied specifically in an economic crisis. Certainly, Keynes was not arguing that governments should always be undertaking massive job creation projects, but rather confining action to those times when the market was unable to correct itself.

Conclusion

In classical economics, markets operate efficiently. Buyers and sellers find a price agreeable to both parties, and goods and services are bought and sold. As long as the state and organised labour do not interfere in the market, growth and prosperity should be available to all, albeit perhaps unevenly distributed. But John Maynard Keynes recognised three aspects of life in an economic downturn that did not seem to fit this idea. First, persistent unemployment, and regular cycles of it, suggested that labour markets are not as efficient as the classical economists thought. Keynes reasoned that this was because wages and prices are 'sticky'. Second, in an economic downturn, entrepreneurs and consumers tend to save money, or pay off debt, as an insurance against harder times in the future. Christened by Keynes as the 'paradox of thrift', Keynes saw that this refusal to spend makes worse the very problem that a struggling economy faces – lower demand for goods and services. This then explains a third issue: that in a depression market mechanisms stumble and there are stocks of unsold goods. Keynes realised that in a long-term economic downturn, entrepreneurs are unlikely to invest in their businesses. Given this, Keynes argued that the state needs to step in and undertake projects that create employment and also leave behind useful infrastructure for private business to make use of once economic recovery begins.

Largely ignored in 1930s Britain, the massive spending Keynes argued for came ultimately in 1939 with the outbreak of the Second World War. In 2020, it was only when scientists predicted a possible tally of coronavirus deaths ten times greater than those in London during the Blitz that the Conservative government turned once more to Keynes' ideas and announced a government spending programme, ending ten years of austerity. It is hard to underestimate the influence upon economic thinking that Keynes had. By focussing on economies as a whole and on demand, Keynes effectively invented macroeconomics. As we will see in the next chapter, Keynes was to have a profound influence on how governments operated in the 30 years after the end of the Second World War, though the 'Treasury View' was never truly defeated and would return. In Chapter Nine we will see that in the era after 1979, neoliberal ideas mapped nicely onto the Treasury View. Even so, as we will see in Chapter Eleven, Keynes' ideas do still have some currency in a crisis, particularly during the 2007–2008 financial crisis and then, after an intervening period of austerity, during the Covid-19 pandemic.

Notes

1 For an overview of the Great Depression and Great Recession see Linda Yueh, *The Great Crashes: Lessons from Global Meltdowns and How to Prevent Them* (London, Penguin, 2023), introduction and chapter 5.

2 George Orwell, *The Road to Wigan Pier* (London, Penguin, 2001); Walter Greenwood, *Love on the Dole* (London, Jonathan Cape, 1974).

3 The most comprehensive biography of Keynes is Robert Skidelsky, *John Maynard Keynes, 1883–1946: Economist, Philosopher, Statesman* (London, Penguin, 2003). This brings together in one volume Skidelsky's three-volume biography of Keynes. For something more focussed on Keynes' application to today see Robert Skidelsky, *Keynes: The Return of the Master* (London, Penguin, 2009). For a quick overview of Keynes see Linda Yueh, *The Great Economists: How Their Ideas Can Help us Today* (London, Viking, 2018), chapter 6. Tough going is the General Theory itself, John Maynard Keynes, *The General Theory of Employment, Interest and Money* (London, BN Publishing, 2008), but chapter 24 which addresses Keynes' thoughts for the future is still interesting and relevant.

4 Nicholas Watt, "David Cameron Beats a Hasty Retreat over Call for Voters to Pay Down Debts", *The Guardian*, 5 October 2011.

5 John Maynard Keynes, *A Tract on Monetary Reform* (London, Macmillan, 1923), 80.

References

Greenwood, W. *Love on the Dole* (London, Jonathan Cape, 1974).

Keynes, J. M. *A Tract on Monetary Reform* (London, Macmillan, 1923).

Keynes, J. M. *The General Theory of Employment, Interest and Money* (London, BN Publishing, 2008).

Orwell, G. *The Road to Wigan Pier* (London, Penguin, 2001).

Skidelsky, R. *John Maynard Keynes, 1883–1946: Economist, Philosopher, Statesman* (London, Penguin, 2003).

Skidelsky, R. *Keynes: The Return of the Master* (London, Penguin, 2009).

Watt, N. "David Cameron Beats a Hasty Retreat over Call for Voters to Pay Down Debts", *The Guardian*, 5 October 2011.

Yueh, L. *The Great Economists: How Their Ideas Can Help us Today* (London, Viking, 2018).

Yueh, L. *The Great Crashes: Lessons from Global Meltdowns and How to Prevent Them* (London, Penguin, 2023).

6

YOU'VE NEVER HAD IT SO GOOD

Social Democracy in Post-War Britain

John Maynard Keynes was, as we saw in the previous chapter, a remarkable economist whose influence on government policy towards recession was profound. His influence was to shift policy away from the free market belief that economies in severe trouble will correct themselves over time, to a belief that the state must act in severe recessions to restore demand. Keynes was an establishment insider. He came from a respectable upper-middle-class family, was educated at Cambridge, and later became bursar of King's College Cambridge. He was a patron of the arts, particularly ballet, and married a well-known ballerina, Lydia Lopokova. Keynes counted amongst his friends fellow members of the literary 'Bloomsbury group', which included writers such as Virginia Woolf and E. M. Forster. Keynes' skills as an economist, and as a civil servant in the India Office between 1906 and 1908, meant that he was in demand during wartime, serving in the Treasury in both the First and Second World Wars. Indeed, in 1942, his war-work led to a peerage and membership of the House of Lords.[1]

In spite of his respectable social and professional position, Keynes' ideas were often too far ahead of their time and therefore not accepted during his lifetime. At the end of the First World War, the Paris Peace Conference of 1919 imposed upon Germany a harsh set of reparations and deprived it of the coal-producing region of the Saarland which was important for German industry. Keynes argued that the reparations

DOI: 10.4324/9781003161950-6

would traumatise the German population and would likely provoke stirrings of resentment that would lead to war. Over 100 years later, historians are still arguing over the consequences of the Paris Peace Conference and the Treaty of Versailles that was signed there. Many historians do not now believe that the reparations played a significant part in the build-up of resentment or Hitler's rise to power. However, Keynes also argued that deliberately taking measures to reduce Germany's industrial capacity would reduce demand not only in Germany but across Europe with negative effects for all. Certainly, the instability of the German economy, leading in the end to the collapse of the post-war Weimar Republic, did play a significant role in the rise to power of the Nazis.

Likewise, whilst Keynes was ahead of his time in his attitudes to the outcome of the First World War, his ideas on government intervention in the economy were only taken up towards the end of his life. Keynes had some luck in influencing policy in the US, where the 'New Deal', designed to provide work during the Depression, had some flavours of Keynes' thinking. It is somewhat ironic that, in the 1930s, the one government that did protect itself against the Depression through a massive injection of government-stimulated demand into the economy was Nazi Germany during its rearmament programme. To be clear, there is no suggestion that Hitler was familiar with Keynes' work, merely that Hitler's policies had the effect Keynes had suggested should be sought for by public works in Britain, albeit ones designed with peaceful ends. In the end, it was Britain's own need to rearm at the end of the 1930s, and then in earnest from 1939 onwards, that created the demand needed in the economy to drag the country out of its recession.

During the Second World War, Keynes played a key role in the Treasury's efforts to finance the war effort. As the war began to come to an end in 1944, Keynes was a central figure in the British delegation's attendance at the Bretton Woods conference in the US, where the West's post-war economic plan was hammered out. With Britain in decline as an economic superpower, Keynes' ambitious plans for reducing inequality across countries were sidelined by the US, which now wanted to use its global economic dominance precisely to take advantage of such inequalities.[2] We will see more about that in Chapter Eight.

The strain of the conference upon Keynes was enormous. His health had been poor during the 1930s, and he had not fully recovered when war broke out. Yet he continued to play a key role in securing Britain's post-war finances. In 1946, whilst at a conference in the US where Keynes was helping to negotiate an Anglo-American loan, he suffered a series of heart attacks. Weeks after returning to Britain, in April 1946, Keynes died at his Tilton country residence. He was relatively young, aged only 62; so young that he predeceased his parents.

Keynes' early death came at just the moment that his ideas were to receive support from the newly elected Labour Government. In this chapter, we chart the rise of social democracy, primarily from the British perspective. It should also be noted that social democratic forms of government existed in most of Western and Northern Europe and in some places have wholly or partially survived. It should be said from the outset though that, whilst much of this movement was considered to be consistent with 'Keynesian economics', what Keynes would have thought of the developments in economic policy after his death is contested.

The Foundations of Social Democracy

In 1942, Arthur Greenwood, a Labour minister without portfolio in Churchill's war cabinet, commissioned Sir William Beveridge, the former Director of the London School of Economics, to write a report outlining the principles that would underpin social security provision in the years after the war. The 'Social Insurance and Allied Services Report', often simply referred to as the Beveridge Report, identified 'Five Giant Evils' that were to be eliminated: Want, Disease, Ignorance, Squalor, and Idleness.[3] Eighty-odd years on, the names of the Giants look a little odd, or indeed judgemental. But they were not meant to be. Beveridge wanted to tackle poverty and ill health, improve and expand educational opportunities, improve housing, and provide job opportunities for those seeking work. After six years of total war, with the country in ruins, the aims were ambitious. They were also achieved with remarkable success.

Until Keynes, mainstream economics had cautioned against large-scale state provision of services, arguing that the state is inherently inefficient and likely to disrupt the market in such a way as to end up failing to achieve its aims. Yet, the Second World War-time economy in Britain was one of cooperation between the state and private enterprise, undertaken on an enormous scale that had delivered a sustained six-year war-winning effort.

The national sentiment in the aftermath of the war was that, if the state could organise for war, then it could organise for peace. Underscoring this was the electoral victory of the Labour Party in 1945, which ousted Churchill. Labour had run on a policy of implementing Beveridge's ideas to create the British welfare state. Keynes had not written about creating a welfare state, and it remains an open question as to whether or not he would have approved of the design that was implemented. But, central to the design was Keynes' belief that the state should act as the final backstop of ensuring the public good, as well as act to supplement and regulate market forces. The policies that were implemented to try to achieve that in the 30-odd years after the Second World War became known as social democracy and stood in sharp contrast to the egocentric small-state economics that had dominated before the war and would again from 1979 onwards.

The Operation of Social Democracy

In mainstream economics, people make decisions about their future and act to fund them accordingly. An 18-year-old might decide to invest in university education in the hope of a return in the form of higher earnings later in life. Someone in work might pay forward into their retirement through a private pension plan. The problem with this, from a social point of view, is that it only recognises and rewards investments in paid labour, and that has a habit of reinforcing inequalities in society. For example, as we saw in Chapter Three, women undertake a disproportionate amount of the domestic labour that is so essential for the continuation of our society – childcare, housework, caring for the elderly, and the like. Because of this they spend time outside of paid employment (and often in lower-paid, fixed-term contracts), the result of which is that they have less to set aside for old age and, therefore, smaller pension pots in retirement. Social democracy tried to address inequality by starting from the principle that those in work should support those that could not work for good reason. Just as children have their education paid for by the collective efforts of those who are older than them and in work, in turn they will pay the cost of education for the next generation. Likewise, the elderly receive pensions paid for by the work of the next generation whom they had paid to educate. This was an economic model built around society, rather than the individual economic agent, and as such it had to have embedded within it some principles as to what society should consist of or set out to achieve.

The methods to implement the safety which social democracy was designed to create, by tackling Beveridge's five 'Giants', were begun in earnest in the first post-war Labour government of 1945–1951.[4] More than that, whilst the Conservatives did undo some of these reforms whilst in office between 1951 and 1964, generally speaking, they too took a social democratic turn. And so, the post-war decades up until the 1980s saw the rollout of social democratic policies. To tackle slum housing, massive public housing projects and slum clearance projects were undertaken. Wythenshawe, the site of the first National Health Service (NHS) hospital, for example, was built to facilitate the slum clearances of central Manchester. In addition to slum clearance, new towns, such as Stevenage and Milton Keynes, were created to provide housing. There was also a sustained effort by councils to provide local housing. By 1979, one-third of Britain's housing stock was social housing.

Addressing the problem of 'Want', schemes were put into place to provide support for those out of work. In Britain, the National Insurance Act (1946) and the National Assistance Act (1948) laid the foundations of the welfare state. They provided for sickness and unemployment benefits, old age pensions, widows' pensions, and maternity and death grants. The workhouse was finally abolished, and responsibility for assisting the poor, unemployed, and elderly moved from local to national government. To tackle 'Disease', the NHS came into being in 1948 with health care free at the point of delivery. Controversially, though, the Labour government rowed back from the principle of universal free health care as early as 1951, when it began to charge people for half the cost of spectacles and false teeth. This led the politician who had driven the formation of the NHS, Aneurin Bevan, to resign from government as he predicted, quite rightly, that by introducing any charges at such an early stage there would be a creep back to charging people for health care. The Conservative government that followed introduced prescription charges in 1952, sparking off a debate about the cost, and extent, of health care provided by the NHS. As we will see in Chapter Ten, this was the beginning of a long road to the privatisation in all but name of the NHS.

Following an Act of 1944, 'Ignorance' was tackled by the provision of free education up to the age of 15. There was also the provision of school meals, some basic medical services, and the introduction of free school milk, so controversially abolished in 1971 by Margaret Thatcher, the then Secretary of State for Education. There was also a massive expansion of the university sector in the 1950s and 1960s with existing university colleges such as Nottingham and Leicester becoming independent institutions (they were formerly colleges of the University of London), and new universities being built such as Sussex, Lancaster, and Warwick. But the route into them was enormously controversial. The school system was divided up as follows: grammar schools could be accessed via examination at age 11 (the 'Eleven-plus'). Those who did not take, or failed, the exam went to new secondary modern schools. The grammar schools fed into universities, whereas the secondary moderns fed into – if anywhere at all – polytechnics which focused on technical subjects, particularly engineering. This system effectively set up a class divide between those who passed the Eleven-plus and those who did not. And so, though it is true that many more people after the Second World War accessed higher education than before, it is hard to know what would have become of those who for whatever reason failed the exam but still had academic potential.

Social Democratic Economic Planning

Social democracy was a collective attempt to help spread risk and moderate uncertainty in life; an attempt to relieve some of the burden on the individual to sustain themselves and their family. But it stretched to more than that. It stood for an accommodation between the state, employers, and workers. It recognised the power which employers had by dint of providing people with the money they needed to sustain themselves. In Germany, for example, this inequality of power was smoothed out from 1951 onwards, requiring large coal and steel companies to provide their workers with 50% rates of representation on their boards. From 1971, this was extended to all firms with over 2000 employees, and today in all firms with headcounts over 500 but fewer than 2000, employers are required to have one-third of board members drawn from their employees. This did not amount to a takeover of firms by workers; companies retained power through controlling the chair's casting vote. But it did give workers a significant stake in the management of the companies in which they worked.

It was not only in Germany where this practice was followed. For example, the 1967 Iron and Steel Act in Britain likewise mandated the presence of worker representatives on the board of British Steel. There were also attempts to organise wages, terms, and conditions at industry level. Following on from Keynes' focus on demand, social democratic states looked at keeping up demand through supporting higher wages. In Britain from 1945 until the late 1980s, wage councils covered a range of industries including catering, clothing production, and retail. At their peak, they covered around 3.5 million workers, and even after the dilution of their powers during the 1980s, before their abolition at the end of the decade, they covered around 2.5 million workers. The councils had powers to set wages and other conditions of employment in the industries they covered. This was important as a minimum wage was not introduced in the UK until 1998. Social democratic states not only concerned themselves with wages, but also, following Keynes, with unemployment. To this end, some states introduced maximum working weeks. France, for example, limited its working week to 39 hours until 2000, when it further reduced the working week to 35 hours in order to create more work and combat high unemployment.[5]

Social democratic states were also content with interfering with private enterprise, either where the motive to generate profit led to lapses in worker safety or where natural monopolies existed. For example, in 1946, a UK Act of Parliament nationalised the coal mining industry. The industry had been government-run in the two World Wars but was otherwise still in private hands. The mining infrastructure needed significant investment to make production cheaper and to improve safety for miners. To this end, the coal mining industry was nationalised, with the responsibility for running the industry handed to the newly formed National Coal Board. In the few years following, a number of natural monopolies were also nationalised, including electricity production and supply, the rail network, the steel industry (which was first nationalised in 1947, privatised again in 1951 by the incoming Conservative government, and eventually renationalised in 1967), and many more. Even the Bank of England, itself sitting on the monopoly that was the supply of money into the economy, was nationalised.

As time went on, the practice of nationalisation in Britain went further than just taking into public ownership natural monopolies. By the 1970s, a number of failing businesses had been nationalised by the British government, including Rolls Royce, British Aerospace (the producer of the iconic Mini car), British Leyland (which later went on to become the Rover Group and parcelled up as a subsidiary of British Aerospace), and British

Shipbuilders. These were undertaken because of the fear of high amounts of localised unemployment in the towns and cities where these industries were chiefly located. It could be said that the concern of a lack of demand in a local area blighted by high unemployment was inspired by Keynes' focus on demand, but this is a long way away from what we saw in the previous chapter. As already noted, it is hard to know what Keynes would have thought about these policies, but it is probably the case that he would not have approved of them.

Government investment in research and development was also a feature of social democratic countries, though it was undertaken in the largely market-driven economy of the US too. Despite the differences between the British and US economies in the 30 years after the Second World War, both invested heavily into the development of technologies that could help to give an upper hand in the Cold War and the Space Race. Driven by the necessity for an upper hand militarily, this relationship between the state and private sector became known as the Military–Industrial Complex. By the end of the 1970s, around 70% of investment in the US's aviation research and development was undertaken by the government. Many of the developments in technology that took place as part of this programme of research and development ultimately had commercial civilian outcomes. Teflon, as a material designed to shield spacecraft from the intense heat of Earth re-entry, happened also to make cooking pans non-stick. The US military's work on developing a diffuse data storage network, one that would not suffer from the dangers of a critical targeted strike, gave rise to the internet.[6] In Britain, the development of nuclear power stations was an offshoot from research and development in nuclear weapons and in nuclear reactors for submarines.

That the British state got so heavily involved in running of industry had the side effect of turning the ability of the state to be commercially successful into a political issue that regularly featured in the press and everyday discussions. As we will see in Chapter Seven, neoliberal economists had argued since the 1940s that the state was inefficient at managing resources in an economy. This came from two premises. The first is the belief that the market allocates resources in the most efficient way, as we saw in Chapters One and Two. The second is that economies are too complex for any one state planner to comprehend and act on. This, as the argument goes, makes it impossible for states to plan economies. (Interestingly, mainstream economics assumes that the individual does have enough perfect market information to plan their own economic activity.) Intertwined with the debate about the state's commercial abilities was a discussion about the extent to which organised labour might be affecting the economy too. Jack Jones, the General Secretary of the Transport and General Workers' Union (now UNITE), was described in 1977 as the 'most powerful man in Britain' after a Gallup poll found that 54% of respondents thought Jones was more powerful than the Prime Minister.[7] We saw in Chapter Four that mainstream economics has always been of the opinion that strong labour organisation can have negative effects on the economy. But more than that, the involvement of trade unions in industrial and economic planning had helped to reduce inequality in Britain. Social democratic welfare and labour policies, including the nationalisation of industries and of firms (for which read: depriving business of monopoly opportunities), led to, by the end of the 1970s, a counteroffensive from businesses, neoliberal economists, and right-wing politicians, who sought to roll back the state's active intervention in the economy. We explore that battle in the next chapter.

The ideas that underpinned the era of social democracy were fairness and security. And whilst the results were far from utopian, there was an increase in the fair distribution of wealth and resources in society by a good number of yardsticks. Social democracy was productive too. Between 1945 and 1973, the UK's GDP growth averaged around 3.8% per annum. Compare this with the period 1992–1997 when it was 2.68%; it later fell to just over 2% in the 2010s. Moreover, social democracy achieved redistributive fairness. From the end of the Second World War until the 1980s, the top 0.1% of earners paid, on average, between 40% and 50% tax on earnings. Today, the top 1% in the UK pay around 30% of their earnings in tax on average, with some paying as low as 11%. In the same period from 1945 to 1980, the share of national income held by the top 0.1% of the populations of the UK, US, and France dropped to rates that were substantially lower than before or after.[8]

Conclusion

From roughly 1945 to 1980, the UK, inspired by the ideas of John Maynard Keynes and William Beveridge, developed a substantial state sector covering everything from health care to university education and even aviation in the form of projects such as Concorde. Two ideas underpinned this. First was Keynes' idea that the state could and should undertake planning within the economy. The logic behind this was simple and popular – if the government could use planning to win the most calamitous war in the history of mankind, then it could plan for a new future in times of peace. Second was the work of Beveridge in addressing the 'Five Giant Evils': Want, Disease, Ignorance, Squalor, and Idleness. Over the course of three decades, inequality was dramatically lowered. But the expansion of the state, and its regulation of the economy, reduced opportunities for business to make money in industries such as health care, which were potentially highly profitable. As we will see in Chapter Nine, when the economy faltered in the late 1970s, classical ideas of organising society returned. Rather than employment being considered a collective endeavour, we returned to the idea that it was the individual's responsibility to, as Norman Tebbit, Thatcher's Employment secretary, is often misquoted as saying, 'get on your bike and get a job'. In the next chapter we turn to the collapse of social democracy and the rise of neoliberalism.

Notes

1   For a biographical insight into Keynes, see Robert Skidelsky, *John Maynard Keynes, 1883–1946: Economist, Philosopher, Statesman* (London, Penguin, 2003).
2   For the transition from British to US economic supremacy and the discussions at Bretton Woods, see Benn Steil, *The Battle of Bretton Woods: John Maynard Keynes, Harry Dexter White and the Making of a New World Order* (Princeton, New Jersey, Princeton University Press, 2013).
3   The Beveridge Report, in effect, laid down the post-war British welfare state. A good history of that is Nicholas Timmins, *The Five Giants: A Biography of the Welfare State* (London, Fontana Press, 1996).
4   For an accessible overview of the Labour governments of 1945–1950 and 1950–1951, see Robert Pearce, *Attlee's Labour Governments, 1945–51* (London, Routledge, 1993).
5   For British and German post-war economic organisation and the firm, see Thomas K. McCraw, *Creating Modern Capitalism: How Entrepreneurs, Companies, and Countries Triumphed in Three Industrial Revolutions* (Cambridge, Massachusetts, Harvard University Press, 1997).
6   For US post-war economic development and the firm, see also Thomas K. McCraw, *Creating Modern Capitalism*; for the role of the state in pushing forward innovation, see Mariana Mazzucato, *The Entrepreneurial State: Debunking Public vs Private Sector Myths* (London, Penguin, 2018).
7   Mark Tran, "Union Leader Jack Jones Dies", *The Guardian*, 22 April 2009.

8 See David Harvey, *A Brief History of Neoliberalism* (Oxford, Oxford University Press, 2008), particularly chapter 1 for a comparison between the two eras.

References

Harvey, D. *A Brief History of Neoliberalism* (Oxford, Oxford University Press, 2008).

Mazzucato, M. *The Entrepreneurial State: Debunking Public vs Private Sector Myths* (London, Penguin, 2018).

McCraw, T. K. *Creating Modern Capitalism: How Entrepreneurs, Companies, and Countries Triumphed in Three Industrial Revolutions* (Cambridge, Massachusetts, Harvard University Press, 1997).

Pearce, R. *Attlee's Labour Governments, 1945–51* (London, Routledge, 1993).

Skidelsky, R. *John Maynard Keynes, 1883–1946: Economist, Philosopher, Statesman* (London, Penguin, 2003).

Steil, B. *The Battle of Bretton Woods: John Maynard Keynes, Harry Dexter White and the Making of a New World Order* (Princeton, New Jersey, Princeton University Press, 2013).

Timmins, N. *The Five Giants: A Biography of the Welfare State* (London, Fontana Press, 1996).

Tran, M. "Union Leader Jack Jones Dies", *The Guardian*, 22 April 2009.

7

SERFDOM, CAPITALISM, AND FREEDOM

Donald Trump's 2016 election campaign rallies often broke out into a chorus of people chanting 'drain the swamp'. Trump's message was that politicians are corrupt and power-hungry, but that he, an entrepreneur, could be trusted with the money in citizens' pockets. Two key ideas lie behind that proposition. First, the idea that the state naturally tends towards authoritarian government. Second, that politicians use the state to further their own ends, not those of the people. Trump presented himself as an outsider to the political class, someone whose self-promoted success from, and belief in, the free market marked him out as having both ideological beliefs and personal qualities that would champion ideas beneficial to ordinary voters. Based on the free market and the small state, we will see that these ideas and the policies that flowed from them can be traced back to the work of Friedrich Hayek and Milton Friedman, both of whom have been influential on the political right and in the popular imagination. To these two and their ideas, we now turn.

As we saw in Chapter Six, Keynes' influence on economics came to bear in the 1940s and, after his death, in 1946, resulted in 30-odd years of social democratic thinking. By contrast, Hayek's influence was eclipsed by Keynes until the 1970s. At the end of the 1970s, the United States and Britain were suffering from economic downturns that combined high inflation, low growth, and high unemployment. For the political right, this was a perfect opportunity to push back against the

DOI: 10.4324/9781003161950-7

socialist-inspired turn to social democracy and place an individualistic conception of economics back into the political mainstream. Hayek and Friedman played a crucial role in this and, indeed, had been preparing for such a moment. First, we look at their ideas and set them against the post-war Keynesian background they were being developed in. Second, we look at how they popularised their ideas so that, when Keynesianism faltered in the 1970s, they were ready to offer small-state, free market solutions attractive to the political right.

Born in Austria at the end of the nineteenth century, Friedrich Hayek had served in the Austrian army in the First World War. After the war, Hayek took up studies in law and political science. In 1929, he was appointed professor at the London School of Economics (LSE). The appointment was not accidental. Despite the synergy between Keynes' ideas and the implementation of the Beveridge Report, it was Beveridge who appointed Hayek in the hopes of establishing a challenge to the economic thinking which Keynes was encouraging at Cambridge. Despite the prestige of the LSE, Hayek struggled to challenge Keynes' dominance of the economics discipline. When the Second World War broke out, Hayek was ineligible for any kind of war service due to having been an enemy combatant during the First World War. He remained at the LSE which, ironically, was evacuated to Cambridge. There is even a story that Keynes and Hayek spent an evening on the roof of the chapel of King's College undertaking fire watch, though there is no record of what was said.[1]

In contrast to Keynes, Hayek focussed on issues of supply. Hayek noticed that when economies were in a recession, central banks often injected more money into the economy by printing cash, holding interest rates low to encourage investment, or a combination of both these methods. Hayek argued that this was a mistake. When money was too readily available, entrepreneurs invested in products which were not necessarily desired by consumers. When these products went unsold, companies went bankrupt, leaving industrial capacity invested where it need not be. In addition, cheap credit incentivised long-term capital investment and Hayek argued that this too was a problem because it limited the possibility of entrepreneurs attempting to realise short-term gains which could kick-start the economy. Resisting the temptation to meddle in the money supply was, for Hayek, crucial to solving the problems of the Great Depression and stood in contrast to Keynes' focus on demand.

The Road to Serfdom

During the Second World War, Hayek set about writing a book that attempted to explain the rise of the interwar authoritarian governments. For Hayek, *The Road to Serfdom*, first published in 1944, was a form of intellectual war-work.[2] Wartime propaganda suggested that there was something inherently warlike about the German national character. Hayek rejected this, focussing instead on economic causes of authoritarian government. Hayek set about tracing the development of the nineteenth-century liberal tradition to identify how, in his opinion, it had been corrupted into the dictatorships of Nazi Germany and Fascist Italy.

In the 1930s (and since), many on the political left argued that interwar fascism was the end point of the development of capitalism. As the economies of countries grew, they looked for new markets, natural resources, and labour. Thinkers such as Rosa Luxemburg and Lenin argued that it was this expansionary process that had led to, first, the carving up of much of the world into the European empires (in particular, the partition of Africa in the late nineteenth century) and, second, bitter rivalry between the European powers, resulting in war.[3] Hayek wanted to counter the argument that the interwar dictatorships were the natural extension of capitalist competition. He argued that it was deviation from the liberal economic tradition that led to fascism. *The Road to Serfdom* was an appeal to the liberal tradition, so much so that Hayek dedicated it to 'Socialists of All Parties'.

In putting his arguments forward, Hayek stood in direct opposition to Keynes. In Chapter Five, we saw Keynes' faith in the role of the state in planning economic development, particularly in times of turmoil. By contrast, Hayek argued that it was planning that had led to authoritarian government. For Hayek, the problem with state planning was that it involved surrendering the responsibility of planning to a single individual. In a bureaucratic system such as the state, Hayek argued, one person had to ultimately decide on what course of action should be taken. That person's judgement would have to be deferred to, and deferred to repeatedly, over a given period of time. In this sense, planning led societies to sleepwalk into dictatorship. The argument was far from abstract; Hayek singled out individuals who supported state planning such as the historian E. H. Carr as 'totalitarians in our midst'.[4]

Not only did Hayek worry about the need for planners to defer to a single individual, but he was also concerned that no one individual could actually make rational choices in regards to economic problems. As we saw in Chapters One and Two, mainstream economics assumes that through prices adjusting, markets tend to equilibrium. Drawing upon the liberal tradition, Hayek argued that markets are extremely complicated networks with millions, if not billions, of transactions, going on all the time. When individuals make choices as to whether or not to buy a good or service, they affect that good or service's price. If it becomes scarce, its price increases. If it becomes plentiful, its price falls. In this way, the free market acts as a kind of constant referendum on the value of goods within an economy, and how they should be distributed. For Hayek, the market represented a form of collective agreement, made amongst all of the people operating in that market, as to the value of particular goods and services. Against the collective wisdom of hundreds, or thousands, or millions of people, no single planner could hope to offer a better estimate of how goods and services should be priced or distributed. Hayek argued that the result of this economic mismanagement would be a society in which all but a few people, close to the top of government, would be poorer.

Hayek argued that by removing the visible hand of the state, and dismantling the state's involvement in the economy, individual liberty would be guaranteed. Hayek praised Adam Smith and argued in favour of ideas we saw in Chapter Two such as removing international trade barriers such as tariffs, and reducing regulation of businesses and financial services. In 2013, these ideas were used by the UK coalition government to commission its so-called 'bonfire of the quangos', the mass culling of bodies funded by the government but not directly controlled by them.[5] The outcome of this was, however, largely negative. For example, the Standards Board for England – which oversaw the investigation of breaches of a Code of Conduct by independent adjudicators – was abolished, and councillors were made responsible for investigating and punishing their own for breaches of standards in public life. In 2021, the Public Accounts Committee published a report which blamed the abolition of boards such as the Standards Board for a lack of transparency and accountability in public bodies. The work of wage councils was, likewise, finally brought to a close with the abolition of the Agricultural Wages Council, which was one of the few statutory bodies left with responsibility for setting wages. But it was this small-state economy which Hayek saw as the guarantee of liberty – liberty from the state's control of the wants of individuals. Hayek placed the relationship between individual liberty and the free market above even democracy itself, which for many is the guarantee of liberty. We'll see more about that in Chapter Eight.

The Road to Serfdom sold well. Its debut run was limited due to the rationing of paper during the Second World War. In March 1944, its first run of 2000 copies sold out straight away and the publisher, Routledge, ordered 2500 more copies. (In the US, the University of Chicago Press published the book.) *The Road to Serfdom* was a success in the US. Upon its first publication, it sold 30,000 copies, and it is estimated to have, as of 2023, sold in total over 400,000 copies in the US alone. But it was less successful in Britain. George Orwell reviewed the book for the *Observer*. Orwell conceded to Hayek that collectivism ran the danger of 'concentration camps, leader worship, and war', but also argued that Hayek's vision of free market capitalism had only brought 'dole queues, the scramble for markets, and war' as an alternative. Orwell felt that unless 'a sense of right and wrong' could be restored to politics, so that collectivism could achieve without dictatorship what free market capitalism had failed to do, the prospects for the future were 'depressing'.[6] Of course, as we have seen, mainstream economics does not have a sense of right or wrong to inject into its philosophy.

Keynes similarly struggled with a sense that *The Road to Serfdom* had established a problem, but not a credible solution. Sailing over the Atlantic to the Bretton Woods conference of 1944, Keynes read a copy of the book, which was supplied to him by Hayek. Writing to Hayek, Keynes, much like a lecturer marking an undergraduate essay, began with praise, calling the work 'a grand book'. But then he moved to his concerns. Keynes argued that more planning, not less, was needed within the economy. Like Orwell, he recognised the issue of morality involved in collective planning, writing that, 'Moderate planning will be safe if those carrying it out are rightly orientated in their own minds and hearts to the moral issue.'[7] Keynes then moved to his main objection. Like Adam Smith, Hayek conceded some role for the state, for example, the provision of laws and courts, a police force and military, some basic assistance for those in need. But just as Smith had not provided an extensive list of what might or might not be acceptable, nor did Hayek. Where should the line between the state and the free market be drawn? 'You [Hayek] agree that the line has to be drawn somewhere... But you give us no guidance whatever on where to draw it.' Then Keynes eviscerated Hayek's work by writing that, once Hayek conceded 'that a line has to be drawn, you are, on your own argument, done for, since you are trying to persuade us that so soon as one moves an inch in the planned direction you are necessarily launched on the slippery path that will lead you in due course over the precipice'.[8] This is an important critique because this is exactly the line which organisations such as the Institute for Economic Affairs and the Adam Smith Institute take whenever the government proposes new economic policies that vary from doubling-down on free market remodelling of the economy.

Where to draw the line was a question that Hayek wrestled with until the publication of *The Constitution of Liberty* in 1960.[9] In the meantime, Hayek went on a tour of the US in late 1944, where his ideas outlined in *The Road to Serfdom* were well met. The *Reader's Digest* even produced a condensed version of the work for him. In early 1950, he accepted a visiting professorship at the University of Arkansas which was based in a state that allowed divorces with little burden of proof of fault and minimal residency qualifications. Once there, Hayek divorced his wife in order to marry his cousin before moving to the University of Chicago where he stayed until 1962. At Chicago, he worked alongside Milton Friedman who was in the School of Economics (Hayek worked on the cross-departmental Committee on Social Thought). We'll see in Chapter Eight that Friedman and colleagues from the Chicago School of Economics were crucial in spreading neoliberal economic policies to other countries such as Chile, and promoting them in the US.

The Mont Pèlerin Society

Whilst Hayek praised Smith's work, *The Road to Serfdom* differed from the liberal tradition by focussing on economic versions of liberty. The broader social purpose that underlay nineteenth-century liberalism, such as J. S. Mill's utilitarianism, was not present in Hayek's individualistic stance on liberty. This put it at odds with the state planning envisaged by Keynes, and the social democratic ideas expressed in the Beveridge Report. During the post-war Keynesian era, Hayek set about laying the foundations of a pushback against state planning. In 1947, he brought together academics, politicians, and business leaders to form the Mont Pèlerin Society. Membership of the club required nomination by two other members, and a sizeable wedge of cash, ensuring that those admitted shared similar views to the existing membership.[10]

Hayek oversaw the development of the society as its president from 1947 to 1961. His first draft of its aims outlined his vision of liberalism as:

> a policy which deliberately adopts competition, markets, and prices as its ordering principles and uses the legal framework provided by the state in order to make competition as effective and beneficial as possible and to supplement it where, and only where, it cannot be made effective.[11]

Alongside Hayek's work establishing the Mont Pèlerin Society, Hayek spent the years after the war writing *The Constitution of Liberty*, as we have seen, to answer Keynes' question as to where the line between the state and the free market should be drawn. Like *The Road to Serfdom*, *The Constitution of Liberty* was highly influential amongst the political right. Both books played a significant role in Hayek being awarded the Nobel Prize in Economics in 1974.

In an anecdote with, admittedly, somewhat apocryphal tinges to it, Margaret Thatcher allegedly withdrew from her handbag a copy of *The Constitution of Liberty* in response to a policy paper on political philosophy presented to her at a Conservative Research Department meeting in 1975. Holding it aloft, Thatcher declared, 'This is what we believe.' Upon her election as Prime Minister in 1979, Thatcher set about implementing free market-based economic policies at the same time as dismantling the social democratic post-war state and the accommodation between the state, employers, and organised labour. So great an influence were Hayek's ideas that they were recognised with two awards of the highest (civilian) honour, the award of the Companion of Honour in the UK and the Medal of Freedom in the US, presented in 1984 and 1991, respectively.

Milton Friedman and *Capitalism and Freedom*

Another scholar at the University of Chicago who strongly influenced the development of free market, neoliberal ideas and their adoption by the political right was Milton Friedman. Friedman was a professor in the School of Economics at Chicago. Like Hayek, his economics proceeded from the idea that market solutions for economic problems were more efficient than those offered by the state. Friedman argued that practically all government interventions in the market led to inefficient allocation of resources in society and were a drag on the creation of wealth.[12]

In *Capitalism and Freedom*, published in 1962, Friedman outlined practical policies for improving the operation of the market to maximise freedom. Whilst his ideas were based on the politics of the US, they were taken up by the political right in many countries. Friedman's ideas centred on the dismantling of the social democratic state. On workers' rights, Friedman argued for the abolition of minimum wage levels. He argued that minimum wage levels in an industry represented a defence of the income of skilled workers at the expense of unskilled workers. By abolishing minimum wage levels, the argument went, unskilled workers who could not get skilled work, or experience that would qualify them for skilled work, would be able to compete for work at the market rate that would be denied to them at, what was assumed to be, an artificially high minimum wage. We saw in Chapter Four how one Tory MP attempted to put this logic to use to argue for the abolition of the UK minimum wage for people with disabilities.

From the perspective of employers, Friedman saw higher rates of income tax as a disincentive for people to maximise production above a certain level. By lowering tax levels, Friedman argued, there would be a greater incentive to work and grow the economy, and more money for investment. (Following on from the classical liberals, the assumption being that all would benefit from this boost of entrepreneurial activity.) This was exactly what the short-lived government of Liz Truss argued when it announced the abolition of the 45p higher income tax band and a reduction of the standard rate from 20p to 19p. The Truss government called this the 'Growth Plan'. It was hailed by the *Mail* as a 'true Tory budget',[13] but as we will see in Chapter Fourteen, the plan foundered on the shores of economic reality, having first wiped billions off UK investments.

To justify lowered rates of income tax, Friedman argued that much of the welfare state should be abolished. Friedman argued against social security schemes on the grounds of classical unemployment – that such schemes create a level at which people have no incentive to work because the state will pay them not to. Friedman argued that welfare should come from philanthropy, somewhat conjuring images of nineteenth-century factory owners deciding who did, or did not, qualify as the deserving poor. Here, Friedman was somewhat contradictory because he also argued that firms had no corporate social responsibility other than to maximise profits for investors. In other words, firms should undertake philanthropy, but only when it pays them to do so (which seems somewhat outside the generally defined view of what charity is). Friedman argued that, because shareholders invest in a firm with the sole intention of realising a profit, managers of firms act fraudulently by spending the investment on anything other than activities that maximise profits.

Yet, despite Friedman's argument that the state should not provide social security, he also argued that there was a natural rate of unemployment, and that, in the long run, the state could not eliminate the natural level of unemployment (whilst Hayek argued that to try to do so would cause inflation). The problem with the idea of the natural rate of unemployment is that no one is particularly sure what the rate actually is. This is very important when looking at how to tackle inflation. As we saw in Chapter Four, full employment (or in this case, unemployment being below the natural rate) can cause inflation. The UK suffered from high levels of inflation from late 2021 well into 2022 and 2023. This inflation was accompanied by a fall in the unemployment rate, which, by late 2022, had fallen back to pre-Covid-19 levels.[14] Despite conceding the role of the energy crisis in causing UK inflation (the UK is heavily reliant on imports of gas and oil which were disrupted by the war between Russia and Ukraine), the Bank of England, in line with the monetary policies we saw in Chapter Four, undertook a policy of raising interest rates in order to create unemployment and reduce demand. By the end of 2022, there was a sharp uptick in the number of redundancies announced by firms, leading, in early 2023, to a rise in the rate of unemployment. At the same time, wage increases – particularly, but not only, in the public sector – began to slow, or, when considered as real wages set against inflation, continued to decline.

With unemployment rising, and wage increases beginning to slow, the ability of workers to bargain collectively seemed to be declining. For example, the communications union (the CWU) presented members with an offer from the Royal Mail Group of a consolidated 6% increase in wages in April 2023, and a further consolidated 2% increase in April 2024 (with an unconsolidated bonus of £500 in 2023).[15] The CWU's General Secretary, Dave Ward, gave interviews to the press indicating that this was the best deal members were likely to get, even though it would not cover inflation – which, in 2022, averaged 9.1% and, in early

2023 for goods, was around 13%. Some members reacted angrily to even being consulted by the union on this sub-inflation offer. In contrast, from the perspective of the Bank of England, monetary policy seemed to be working. The Bank steadily raised interest rates from late 2020 to mid-2023. By September 2023, the rate stood at 5.25% and the Bank predicted that inflation would fall back to an average of 6.1% for the year 2023. The policy of creating unemployment to tackle inflation had, it seemed, cut demand and caused unemployment to rise above the natural rate. Given that there is no practical definition of it, only time will tell if the economy was at the natural rate of unemployment, needing an increase in the bank rate to combat it. The winter of 2022–2023 was reasonably mild, leading to a fall in wholesale energy prices, and it may well be factors such as these that have acted on inflation. If so, unemployment could continue to rise throughout 2023 and into 2024 as the effect of interest rate rises plays through. The result would then be a recession.

All of this matters because it was Hayek and Friedman who warned of the inflationary dangers of government spending and wage increases bargained above the market rate by trade unions. This is why the Conservative government was prepared to disrupt people's lives significantly by refusing to grant pay rises demanded by, for example, teachers, nurses, and doctors. Whilst it is true that it was subsequent generations of economists who tied down the theory on this, from the point of view of the popular right, this small-state, anti-union vision of economics goes back to Hayek and Friedman.

Friedman took up the idea that trade unions could disrupt the market for wages, forcing wages higher than employers were prepared to pay and causing unemployment. In an argument similar to his position on minimum wages, Friedman suggested that trade unions benefitted the skilled workers over the unskilled. This was because, so the argument goes, trade unions seek to create barriers to entry into skilled work. Friedman argued that the two most successful trade unions in the US were those that represented airline pilots and those that represented doctors. Working from the laws of supply and demand, Friedman put forward that in imposing restrictions on entry into a profession, trade unions kept the supply of skilled work lower than it otherwise would be. This was another part of Friedman's argument over the abolition of licensing for medical doctors, which we first encountered in Chapter Two.

Friedman was also dismissive of trade unions for two other reasons. First, he was cynical about what he perceived to be the high salaries of union officials (placing him in an odd ideological alliance with the Trotskyite left). Second, he saw trade unions who organised in the public sector to be a disruption in the relationship between buyer and seller. Ordinarily, buyer and seller exchange with each other, stipulating what the seller is willing to offer and what the buyer is willing to pay. But Friedman disliked the way in which the government acted as an intermediary – taking taxes to pay its employees, and so breaking the direct relationship between buyer and seller. Friedman argued that, worse still, governments that saw there to be votes in supporting organised labour would be inclined to pay demands in return for votes (if Friedman was right, the opposite must be true, which might well explain why the Conservatives tend not to meet the demands of teachers and nurses).

The idea that government might act not in the best interests of citizens, but in their own self-interest to gain votes, was brought together into a unified theory by James M. Buchanan, who won the Nobel Prize for economics in 1986 for his work on public choice theory. Buchanan argued that politicians were likely to favour those projects which would secure them votes, rather than those that would best benefit the public good.

The neoliberal pushback against social democracy united three concepts: first, the belief that free markets were efficient whilst the state is not; second, the idea that politicians act in their own interests, which do not always align with those of the general public; third, that the free market was a better guarantor of liberty than anything else. Yet it had to wait for its moment to influence policy in countries such as Britain and the US. This opportunity came in the 1970s with the onset of stagflation.

Opportunity Knocks: 1970s Stagflation and the turn to Neoliberalism

We'll see in Chapter Eight that neoliberal ideas had been forced upon various countries in South America and elsewhere in the years after the Second World War. But in Northern and Western Europe and North America, they struggled to gain popularity in the era of social democracy. As we have seen, Hayek, Friedman, and others had been gathering support for neoliberal ideas amongst businesspeople and the political right. The moment for these ideas came during the latter part of the 1970s. In both the US and Britain, inflation and unemployment were running high whilst growth was sluggish. In theory, this should not have been possible. We have seen that in more recent times of high inflation, governments or central banks will raise interest rates to create unemployment and reduce demand. In 1977 in Britain, unemployment was running at 6% of the working population, a height not seen since the Great Depression of the 1930s. In the same year, inflation was running at around 16%, admittedly down from an eye-watering high of nearly 25% in 1975 (for context, remember that central banks today try to keep inflation at around 2%).

In the same way that the rise in inflation beginning in 2022 was caused by the Russia–Ukraine war and subsequent oil supply issues, inflation in the 1970s was driven by increased costs. In particular, in 1973, the Organisation of Arab Petroleum Exporting Countries, led by Saudi Arabia, declared an oil embargo against those countries which had supported Israel during the Yom Kippur War of October 1973. Britain and the US were targeted, but so too were Canada, Japan, the Netherlands, Rhodesia, South Africa, and Portugal. The result was a 300% increase in the price of oil. Worse still, in 1979, the Iranian revolution led to a decrease in oil production in Iran, forcing up global prices, this time by around 200%. As the cost of oil pushed up prices, organised labour campaigned for higher wages. At the same time, governments focussed on trying to increase growth through investment, rather than raising interest rates which would risk making unemployment even worse. But with growth remaining sluggish, discontent rose as price increases outstripped wage increases, resulting in substantial real wage decreases.

With Keynesian economics seemingly in a shambles, this was the moment for neoliberal policies to move to the fore. Friedman advocated increasing interest rates to batter down inflation. At the same time, the newly elected government of Margaret Thatcher reined in spending, running surpluses in Britain in the early 1980s. The government also reduced income taxes, whilst shifting tax onto consumption, raising VAT paid on non-essentials. (It is worth noting that taxes on consumption hit the poorest hardest.) There was also an attempt to implement Friedman's idea of monetarism, which held that limiting the quantity of money in the economy would limit inflation. This directly challenged government buyouts of firms and maintaining higher levels of unemployment insurance. But this part of the experiment proved somewhat unsuccessful and was abandoned. In the end, it wasn't the elegant economic theory of monetarism that curbed inflation, but unemployment the like of which had not been seen since the Great Depression. More than that, what was important was that the Thatcher and Reagan governments established the idea that good economic policy used unemployment to control inflation; did not seek to get to full employment; shifted tax from the entrepreneur to the worker; and reduced state expenditure in an economic crisis. It was this philosophy that, from 2010 onwards, underpinned the reaction in the UK of, first, the coalition government, and then the Conservative government to the 2007–2008 financial crisis, the disastrous outcome of which we'll see in Chapter Twelve.

Conclusion

In the 1981 episode of 'Yes Minister' called 'The Quality of Life', there is an exchange between Sir Humphrey Appleby, the minister's permanent secretary, and Sir Desmond Glazebrook, chair of the Bank of England. Sir Desmond confesses to not understanding economics. To a bewildered-looking Sir Humphrey, he laments:

> 'It took me thirty years just to understand Keynes' economics, then just when I'd cottoned on, everyone started getting hooked on these new monetarist ideas. You know, "I Want to be Free" by Milton Shillman.'
> 'Milton Friedman,' corrects Sir Humphrey.
> 'Why are they all called Milton?' replies Sir Desmond tetchily.
> 'Anyhow, I've only got as far as Milton Keynes.'
> 'Maynard Keynes,' says Sir Humphrey.
> 'I'm sure there's a Milton Keynes?' replies Sir Desmond.
> 'Well, yes there is, but, it, erm.'

With Sir Humphrey at a loss, they change subjects.[16]

Looking back from 40 years on, it looks strange that a prime-time comedy could make a joke about the battle for supremacy between two economic schools of thought and get a laugh. That it did is testament to how much of a sea-change the shift from social democratic to neoliberal thought was. It would take years for the policy implications of this change to work through, reshaping Britain in ways we will see in future chapters. But the war over which ideas would rule us was won at around the time Margaret Thatcher was entering power in 1979, and the victory was the result of a much longer debate over what is seen as good economics, as we have seen throughout this book so far – with good economics being cast as the economics of the individual, not the collective.

In 2010, when the US government introduced the Patient Protection and Affordable Care Act (otherwise known as Obamacare), Hayek's 1944 book, *The Road to Serfdom*, leapt to the top of the Amazon bestseller list. Little surprise; we've seen that Hayek's book is a popular account of how state planning and involvement in the economy 'naturally' tends to dictatorships of the type seen in interwar Germany and Italy. For the US right, looking for intellectual tools with which to attack Obama, Hayek provided a ready-made critique. As for the idea that politicians act selfishly, we can see that this is embedded in economics' conception of the self-interested economic agent. For Friedman, and advocates of public choice theory, politicians use the state to extract money from entrepreneurs and society more broadly in order to favour their specific electoral base and, therefore, ensure re-election. These ideas, taken together with mainstream economics, have come to be known as 'neoliberalism' – like classical economic thinking, but enhanced by new ideas reflecting developments since the classical era of the early nineteenth century. Taken together, the belief that the state is inherently authoritarian and that its politicians are corrupt justifies state inaction at precisely the wrong moment, such as an economic crisis or natural disaster, as well as encouraging economic policies that benefit business over workers. We'll see more about this soon, but now we turn to how neoliberal ideas became established worldwide, not just in the UK and US.

Notes

1 This story is recounted in Nicholas Wapshott, *Keynes Hayek: The Clash That Defined Modern Economics* (New York, W. W. Norton, 2011), which does a good job of contrasting Keynes and Hayek's ideas; for a shorter introduction to Hayek see Linda Yueh, *The Great Economists: How Their Ideas Can Help us Today* (London, Viking, 2018), chapter 8.

2 Friedrich August Hayek, *The Road to Serfdom* (London, Routledge, 1962).

3 See Chapter Eight for more on this.
4 Hayek, *Road to Serfdom*, chapter 13.
5 Andrew Sparrow, "100 Quangos Abolished in Cost-Cutting Bonfire", *The Guardian*, 22 August 2012.
6 George Orwell, "Review of The Road to Serfdom", in Sonia Orwell and Ian Angus (eds), *The Collected Essays, Journalism and Letters of George Orwell*, Vol. 3 (London, Penguin, 1982), 142–144.
7 Wapshott, *Keynes Hayek*, 200.
8 Ibid.
9 Friedrich August Hayek, *The Constitution of Liberty* (Chicago, Chicago University Press, 1960).
10 For the Mont Pelerin Society there is the society's official history, Ronald Max Hartwell, *A History of the Mont Pelerin Society* (Indianapolis, Liberty Fund Inc., 1995); Richard Cockett, *Thinking the Unthinkable: Think Tanks and the Economic Counter-Revolution 1931–1983* (London, Harper Collins, 1995); critically tracing the influence of the ideas of the society there is Philip Mirowski and Dieter Plehwe, eds., *The Road from Mont Pelerin: The Making of the Neoliberal Thought Collective* (Cambridge, Massachusetts, Harvard University Press, 2009).
11 Hartwell, *The Mont Pelerin Society*, 49.
12 For Friedman's views of the application of his ideas to policy, see Milton Friedman, *Capitalism and Freedom* (Chicago, Chicago University Press, 1962); for an overview of Friedman see Yueh, *The Great Economists*, chapter 10.
13 Jason Groves, "At Last! A True Tory Budget", *Daily Mail*, 24 September 2022.
14 The UK Office of National Statistics publishes a broad range of useful stats for assessing the economy, including inflation and unemployment, see http s://www.ons.gov.uk/.
15 Julia Kollewe and Alex Lawson, "Royal Mail Agrees upon Pay Deal with Postal Workers Union", *The Guardian*, 21 April 2023.
16 Yes Minister. 1981. Season 2, Episode 6, "The Quality of Life". Directed by Peter Whitmore. Aired 30 March, on BBC.

References

Cockett, R. *Thinking the Unthinkable: Think Tanks and the Economic Counter-Revolution 1931–1983* (London, Harper Collins, 1995).
Friedman, M. *Capitalism and Freedom* (Chicago, Chicago University Press, 1962).
Groves, J. "At Last! A True Tory Budget", *Daily Mail*, 24 September 2022.
Hartwell, R. M. *A History of the Mont Pelerin Society* (Indianapolis, Liberty Fund Inc., 1995).
Hayek, F. A. *The Constitution of Liberty* (Chicago, Chicago University Press, 1960).
Hayek, F. A. *The Road to Serfdom* (London, Routledge, 1962).
Kollewe, J. and Lawson, A. "Royal Mail Agrees upon Pay Deal with Postal Workers Union", *The Guardian*, 21 April 2023.

Mirowski, P. and Plehwe, D., eds. *The Road from Mont Pelerin: The Making of the Neoliberal Thought Collective* (Cambridge, Massachusetts, Harvard University Press, 2009).

Orwell, G. "Review of the Road to Serfdom" in Orwell, S. and Angus, I., eds. *The Collected Essays, Journalism and Letters of George Orwell*, Vol. 3 (London, Penguin, 1982), 142–144.

Sparrow, A. "100 Quangos Abolished in Cost-Cutting Bonfire", *The Guardian*, 22 August 2012.

Wapshott, N. *Keynes Hayek: The Clash That Defined Modern Economics* (New York, W. W. Norton, 2011).

Yueh, L. *The Great Economists: How Their Ideas Can Help us Today* (London, Viking, 2018).

8

IMPERIALISM FOR FREE TRADE

Economics is not a science. We will see more about this in Chapter Thirteen. Whereas in science, advances in knowledge and discoveries of new phenomena render obsolete older theories, there are many branches of investigation in economics that, whilst often not compatible with each other, do not 'disprove' each other either. So, whilst social democracy managed to displace the free trade, small-state economics of the pre-Second World War era, it had not dealt it a mortal blow. In Britain, and around the world, for example in Western Europe and North America, managed economies – where the state, businesses, and worker's organisations came together to plan out economic objectives – were popular. Even in Britain, the Conservative Party came to support the NHS for some time, rather than seeking to dismantle it, when they gained power after the 1951 general election.

In those countries in which it was implemented, the era of social democracy reduced the opportunity for unbridled money-making. As we saw in Chapter Six, higher marginal tax rates, nationalisation of monopolies, and government regulation of terms and conditions of employment, including pay, reduced profit margins. Indeed, in the 30 years after the Second World War, in the UK and many other places, economic inequality was reduced to a level lower than ever observed before or since. Even the US, which did not go far down the path of social democracy compared to, say, Britain, France, or the Scandinavian

DOI: 10.4324/9781003161950-8

countries, saw the gap between the incomes of the top and bottom of the earning spectrum narrow.[1] Faced with this, business looked elsewhere to make profits. Even in the age of social democracy, it could still find friends in government who were ready to assist. This chapter looks at the way in which mainstream economic ideas were modified in the post-war years to create neoliberal economies outside of the social democratic countries.

Imperialism, the Highest Stage of Capitalism?

We saw in Chapter Three Marx's ideas on exploitation. Writing in the nineteenth century, Marx also witnessed, alongside the development of industrial capitalism, the growth of the European empires. Marx managed to complete three volumes of his detailed analysis of the operation of capitalism, *Das Kapital*, before his death. In total, Marx had envisaged six volumes in the series. Sadly for us, he died before writing the fourth volume, which was to cover the operation of imperialism. Sadly because, if we had Marx's writing on the subject, a lot of arguing over what Marx would have thought about imperialism could have been avoided.[2]

The focus of those commentators that followed in the tradition of Marx's ideas was on the issue of markets, natural resources, and labour. Lenin wrote that imperialism was the 'highest stage of capitalism' and other influential thinkers such as Rosa Luxemburg followed suit. Much as Marx had, they took the principles of economics and turned them on their head. At the heart of classical economics was the idea of perpetual growth. Lenin and Luxemburg pointed out that perpetual growth had limits within a national economy. Eventually, all labour and resources would be mobilised into production meaning new markets and fresh labour would be required. This led, they argued, to states seeking to expand in order to find more markets, labour, and raw materials. In addition, finance capital needed investment opportunities overseas to counter falling returns on investments at home. There certainly was good reason to believe this. For example, by the latter part of the nineteenth century, Britain was importing much of its raw cotton from India to supply the cotton-hungry textile mills that had fuelled Britain's industrial revolution and made it the world's first superpower.

Whilst the Marxist tradition saw empire as central to capitalism, liberal economists and politicians were sceptical of the benefits of empire.

As we saw in Chapter Two, they believed that the wealth of nations lay in free trade rather than in protectionism. It was in that tradition that politicians such as Richard Cobden and John Bright had argued for the repeal of the Corn Laws, which existed to protect the price of British domestic corn against imports by, at first, setting a price below which corn could not be imported, and later by prohibitive tariffs. This ensured that domestic grain growers maintained their incomes. In so doing, the profits of Britain's aristocratic landed elite were guaranteed at the expense of cheap bread for the working class. Likewise, to encourage imperial trade, a series of Navigation Acts required goods that were to be traded in the empire to be transhipped via Britain. By the end of the 1840s, free trade had won out and both the Corn Laws and the Navigation Acts were repealed. Liberals often argued that the empire was expensive and often caused more problems than it solved. Adam Smith, for example, argued that Britain should return Gibraltar to Spain on the basis that Britain's occupation of Gibraltar had brought together Spain and France as close allies which, otherwise, they would not have been (though this can be debated). Later on, Cobden also argued that British commercial interests in the Mediterranean would have been served better without Gibraltar, rather than with it. This was on the basis that free trade was a better proposition for British business than illicitly introducing goods into Europe through Gibraltar's free port. This all chimes with Ricardo, whom we met in Chapter Two.

For Marxists, imperialism was all about economic greed. And for liberals, free trade was the antidote to imperialism. Both sets of ideas turned out to be both half right and half wrong. In 1953, John Gallagher and Ronald Robinson wrote a short article called 'The Imperialism of Free Trade'.[3] Fifteen pages long, with few footnotes, yet the ideas within are still debated today. Gallagher and Robinson pointed out that the vast majority of overseas investments actually went outside of the empire. This suggested that the empire was not as essential for British business as Marxists had argued.

For Gallagher and Robinson, the focus was not so much on what resources were available outside of Britain but rather on the willingness of people out there to trade on terms preferential to British industry and finance capital. In Argentina, for example, British firms built and controlled the extensive rail network that was central to Argentinian overseas trade. Argentina's political and economic elites welcomed the opportunities for trade and profit which Britain's investment in the country brought. Likewise, the markets for British steel and railway rolling stock were healthy, and returns on financial investments in the Argentinian rail network profitable. As Gallagher and Robinson put it, 'refusals to annex [were] no proof of reluctance to control'. Britain's economic dominance in Argentina, facilitated through the collaboration of local elites, negated any need to consider a costly annexation.

As Britain sought to find outlets for its expanding economy, it looked to control areas into which its economy could expand. Local collaboration was key to how Britain would view an economy. This happened best where local elites were of British descent, such as in the so-called 'white dominions' of Canada, New Zealand, Australia, South Africa, the Irish Free State, and Newfoundland. These colonies were moved to 'dominion' status, allowing them internal self-government long before Britain's other colonies. But outside of the empire, such as in Argentina, what Britain wanted was to use local elites to remove trade barriers, allowing free trade between Britain and economies with resources and markets it wanted to move into. This is not to dismiss the extent of Britain's formal empire, nor the consequences of it for those not part of the local elites, but the pink bits on the map were, as Gallagher and Robinson put it, the 'tip of the iceberg'.[4]

But just as Gallagher and Robinson's vision of how Britain's economy worked upset the Marxist approach to imperialism, it also unsettled the liberal one. Whereas liberals saw free trade as a force for liberation, Gallagher and Robinson demonstrated that it was a means of control. Indeed, Britain's preferred means of control. Not only was free trade a way of leveraging markets, it also allowed for a small state in Britain. The empire's administrative centre in Britain, the Colonial Office, was not a particularly big government department. Debates in the House of Commons that focussed on the empire were poorly attended. Tellingly, the Colonial Office held far less power in British government than the Board of Trade or the Treasury.

Writing in 1953, Gallagher and Robinson were witnessing the end of an era. Britain's overseas empire was being quickly dismantled and more worrying for its global power was the diminishing value of British trade compared to that of the US. The US may well have been founded on anti-colonial ideas, but in the era since the Second World War it has pressured countries to open their markets to US trade and investment using similar tactics to British capitalism in the period before 1945.[5] We turn to this now.

Failures of Collaboration

Gallagher and Robinson could have called their article 'Imperialism *for* Free Trade'. After the Second World War, the US acted to secure its economic interests overseas, principally by imposing free trade on other economies and resisting the closure of markets. To take an early example, in 1951 in Guatemala, a socialist government was elected under the premiership of Jacobo Arbenz. Like many South American governments in the post-1945 era, Arbenz's government was interested in land reform. In particular, they wanted to nationalise private land for redistribution. This was a significant threat to the business interests of the US company United Fruit who held substantial land in Guatemala. United Fruit began lobbying the US government, arguing that this was a gateway to a wave of communist revolutions in South America. Such lobbying was helped by the fact that the US Secretary of State, John Foster Dulles, had been employed by United Fruit earlier in his career, whilst Dulles' brother was the head of the Central Intelligence Agency (CIA). Working with rebels in exile from Guatemala, the US helped to arm them in order to land an invasion. Supplied with US fighter pilots, radio propaganda, and equipment to block government radio communications, the rebels launched an assault in June 1954. As it happened, this assault became somewhat farcical. But it did have the effect of convincing some generals in the Guatemalan military that without US support, the Arbenz government was doomed. As such, they proposed the installation of a former army general who was amenable to working with the US as president. The land reform proposals were soon abolished, safeguarding US business interests in Guatemala.[6]

Working to establish regimes that welcomed US capital has, perhaps, become most identified with the story of the overthrow of the government of Salvador Allende in Chile in the early 1970s. The crisis in Chile was set against the backdrop of the adoption of social democratic and Keynesian economic policies in Chile, Uruguay, Brazil, and Paraguay. Being relatively rich in oil, these countries, known as the Southern Cone countries, were able to prioritise trade with each other and worked to reduce their dependence on the US and Europe for imports. Heavy regulation of key industries, alongside nationalisation of resources such as the mineral extraction industry, allowed governments to spend money on social democratic policies that dramatically reduced inequality. For example, literacy levels in Uruguay reached an unprecedented 95% in the 1960s.

As long ago as the nineteenth century, the US had set a firm embargo against European powers extending their formal empires in South America. As we have seen, Britain's informal interests in Argentina meant that there was no need to break this embargo. However, the Southern Cone countries, an area in which the US had always considered its economic interests to be paramount, were creating an economic environment that was inhospitable to US business. In the case of Chile, in 1968 alone, and at 1968 prices, the copper industry was worth $7.3 billion and was largely owned by US capital. The US telecommunications company ITT held a majority share in the Chilean telecommunications network.[7] When Allende's government threatened to nationalise these two industries, the US saw it as necessary to reconfigure the Chilean economy to a neoliberal model.

The search for collaborators amenable to US business in Chile led to the Chilean military, the National Association of Manufacturers (who just so happened to be part-funded by the CIA and multinational companies), and the broader business community in Chile. A US-backed coup brought down Allende's government in September 1973. The military took over political control of the country under the dictatorship of General Augusto Pinochet. And Pinochet undertook a programme of neoliberalising the country's economy. We saw in Chapter Seven that the leading neoliberal economics department in the US was the University of Chicago Department of Economics, at which Milton Friedman was a professor. In the 1960s, Friedman had participated in a programme to train Chilean economics students in the neoliberal tradition. The students had come to Chicago to undertake postgraduate work in the hope that they would return to Chile and help bring neoliberal economic ideas into the mainstream. However, they got little purchase until the coup, when Pinochet brought into government many of the 'Chicago boys' to implement neoliberal economic policies.

Here we come to the crucial difference between neoliberal economics and the pre-war small-state economics of the classical tradition. It is true that neoliberal economics, the ideas of which now underpin our economics world, held many of the main tenets of the classical school: the small state; the free market; free trade; the operation of the invisible hand. But, of course, it was operating in the era after Keynes' work and the social democratic revolution in economic thinking that Keynes had ushered in. Because of this, neoliberal economic thinking needed something in addition to the classical school – it needed to have ideas, justifications, and methods to break up the social democratic states that had formed around the world. The ideas came readily from the classical school, but the methods were distinctly political. Hayek won the Nobel Prize for economics, not for his academic economics, but rather for the influence of *The Road to Serfdom* on public perceptions of good – and dangerous – economics.[8] Friedman made regular public appearances in lecture tours, television and radio interviews, and newspaper articles. These 'public economists' served to bring neoliberal ideas to the mainstream and to forgive aspects of their implementation that seemed contradictory to the ideas of liberalism and freedom. For example, as we saw in Chapter Seven, Hayek believed that the free market was more important to individual liberty than the existence of a system of political democracy. It was on this basis that Hayek argued that Pinochet's Chile involved greater freedom in its government than Allende's had.[9]

Was it true that Pinochet's dictatorship was more liberal than Allende's democratically elected government? By Hayek's reckoning, yes – Pinochet had introduced a radical market, free from 'excessive' regulation and heavily integrated into the global economy, most notably with the US. But around this time, we see mainstream economics used to justify things well beyond the intended remit of any economist's ideas. Take for example Pinochet's policies towards trade unions in Chile. Trade union organising was subject to extremely strong curbs throughout Pinochet's dictatorship. We saw in Chapter Four that mainstream economics argues that this is consistent to maintaining the free market and a healthy economy. But Pinochet went much further than any economist had cast their net, imprisoning those trade unionists which his regime saw as 'dangerous Marxists'. Those imprisoned were routinely subjected to extreme torture. In the end, it is estimated that more than 40,000 people were tortured and over 2,000 executed.

The torture of trade union activists was not so much about economics, but the context of the Cold War and the existence of authoritarian politics in South American countries, but also elsewhere – even, in the European case, Portugal and Spain until 1974 and 1975, respectively. Eventually, all four of the Southern Cone countries were subject to dictatorships, the economic outcome of them all being the establishment of neoliberal economic policies that favoured the US' economy. It would be fanciful to suggest that economists such as Hayek and Friedman did not know about Chile's human rights abuses; they had both visited as well as studied the country under Pinochet. But there is scant evidence to suggest they approved of them either. Yet, it cannot be ignored that the desire of US business and the support of the US government to establish an economy that was favourable to US business interests, and configured around neoliberal economic ideas, were a major cause of the human rights abuses.

The Washington Consensus

We will see in Chapter Nine that after around 1979, neoliberal ideas were imposed by the political right within social democracies and eventually these ideas moved into the mainstream. Outside of those countries, the desire to reconfigure economies in the neoliberal mould was relentless. One way to do this using economic leverage, rather than force, was through the imposition of neoliberal terms offered to states that found themselves in financial trouble and requiring assistance from the World Bank (WB) or the International Monetary Fund (IMF) (20% of the voting power of the IMF is controlled by the US and Britain alone). In 1989, the US economist John Williamson coined the term 'Washington Consensus'. The consensus was a set of policies that needed to be adopted by countries looking for a bailout from the IMF. These policies are very recognisably neoliberal in their thinking and include: trade liberalisation; tax reform (where reform means shifting from direct to indirect taxes, to the benefit of richer people and business); reduction in state spending; the privatisation of state industries; and opening up industries to overseas investment.

One standout example of these policies being enforced in return for cash is that of Greece since 2010, which has accepted three bailouts funded by the IMF, the European Commission, and the European Central Bank (known as the Troika). These bailouts took place in the aftermath of the 2007–2008 financial crisis, but its origins went back to when Greece had joined the Euro. In order to meet the conditions required to join the Euro, which it could not do legitimately, the Greek government had been systematically returning fraudulent statistics relating to government debt and borrowing. This continued in the decade after joining the Euro. The financial crisis of 2007–2008 revealed that, rather than debt and borrowing being manageable, Greece was in serious financial trouble.[10]

The problem for Greece was that the traditional approach to tackling a serious financial crisis is for a country to allow its currency to depreciate (lose value compared to other currencies). This then makes the cost of domestically produced goods cheaper to overseas buyers, who then are likely to buy more goods or services (in particular, for a country like Greece, this might take the form of more people going on holiday there). But this could not happen because Greece had joined the Euro, and the exchange rate of the Euro is managed centrally by the European Central Bank. The problem for the German and French governments was that much of the Greek bad-debt was held by their banks. Greek membership of the Euro meant that faith in Greece's ability to pay back its debt to its creditors was higher than it should have been. Creditors believed that Greek debt would ultimately be underwritten by the other members of the Euro, in effect making the risk involved more like that of French or German government debt, rather than the debt of a country on the eve of defaulting.

For the German and French governments, writing off Greece's debt was not an option. Nor was allowing Greece to leave the Euro and default given the heavy losses French and German banks would sustain at a moment of deep financial crisis. Greece was pressured to take loans in order to pay back its debts. In 2010, the Troika loaned Greece €110 billion, in 2012 €130 billion, and in 2015 a further €86 billion. The conditions placed on these loans were very much in keeping with the ideas of the 'Washington Consensus' and neoliberal ideas more broadly. For example, in 2012 the Greek government had to agree that no matter which political party won the country's next general election, the terms of the bailout deals would be honoured. This, in effect, put Greece's creditors in charge of Greece's political destiny because it deprived voters of any option to change government policy towards the debt. As a practical symbol of this, officials from the IMF and European Central Bank were placed in Greek ministries to ensure that the Troika's interests were being protected. So much for the Hayek-inspired vision of free market reform leading away from serfdom.

In addition to guarantees over repaying the loans, the Greek government was obliged to undertake economic reforms along the lines of the Washington Consensus. Cutting government expenditure at a time of economic crisis had the effect that we would expect having reviewed Keynes' ideas – the economy shrank yet further, causing significant unemployment. At one stage, Greek youth unemployment hit an eye-watering 65%. Despite this, benefits to support the unemployed were slashed leaving hundreds of thousands with no support at all. Key assets in Greece's infrastructure were privatised, such as ports. Regulated markets such as health care were deregulated and opened up to foreign direct investment. It was not only Greece that saw major neoliberal reforms in return for financial assistance. In the aftermath of the financial crisis of 2007–2008, Ireland found itself in need of IMF cash. After accepting €64 billion from the IMF and EU, the Irish government was forced into a number of neoliberal reforms which included a reduction in public sector pensions, a reduction in the minimum wage (with a resulting negative effect on demand), and deregulation in its health care industry.

Conclusion

Expanding economies look for areas to expand into. But unlike the arguments of Lenin and Luxemburg, we can see here that the preferred way of making this happen is not to invade and impose upon a country a new economic system. Instead, expanding economies look to reconfigure those around them in such a way as to be beneficial to their business interests. In countries such as Guatemala, Chile, and Argentina, social democratic governments were toppled in favour of free market states, often led by military dictators. In the case of Chile, Friedman even trained economists to help the Pinochet government implement free market economic reforms. These coups took place against the backdrop of the Cold War, with the US often working with local elites, the military, and business to impose neoliberal ideas in place of social democratic ones – using tactics with which nineteenth-century British imperialists would have readily identified. However, formal interventions such as those in Vietnam and Korea were costly and controversial. Where possible, the US preferred to bring pressure to bear on countries to reform through informal means. As part of the Washington Consensus, countries ranging from Britain in the 1970s to Greece in 2010 have been forced to implement neoliberal economic ideas that have led to vast profits for entrepreneurs but at the expense of heightened inequality, declining living standards, and severe consequences for mental and physical health. In the next chapter, we look at how neoliberal economic ideas were imposed on the UK economy at the expense of social democracy.

Notes

1 For an excellent account of social democracy in Scandinavia, specifically Sweden, see Avner Offer and Gabriel Soderberg, *The Nobel Factor: The Prize in Economics, Social Democracy and the Market Turn* (Princeton, New Jersey, Princeton University Press, 2016), chapter 8.
2 For a fuller examination of the themes in this chapter, see Jo Grady and Chris Grocott, eds., *The Continuing Imperialism of Free Trade: Developments, Trends and the Role of Supranational Agents* (London, Routledge, 2019); Chris Grocott and Jo Grady, "'Naked Abroad': The Continuing Imperialism of Free Trade", *Capital and Class* 38, no. 3: 541–562.
3 John Gallagher and Ronald Robinson, "The Imperialism of Free Trade", *Economic History Review* 6, no. 1: 1–15.
4 On collaboration, see Ronald Robinson, "Non-European Foundations of European Imperialism: Sketch for a Theory of Collaboration" in Roger Owen, ed., *Studies in the Theory of Imperialism* (London, Longman, 1972), 117–142.
5 It's also the case that despite its anti-colonial origins, within the North American continent the US was a settler-colonial state, see Grocott and Grady, "'Naked Abroad': The Continuing Imperialism of Free Trade".
6 For an account of the coup in Guatemala, see Daniel Litvin, *Empires of Profit: Commerce, Conquest, and Corporate Responsibility* (New York, Texere, 2003).
7 For an account of the Chilean coup, see David Harvey, *A Brief History of Neoliberalism* (Oxford, Oxford University Press, 2008).
8 For the Nobel Prize, see Offer and Soderberg, *The Nobel Factor*.
9 Letter from Friedrich August Hayek to *The Times*, 3 August 1978.
10 An excellent account of the Greek crisis by one of the country's former finance ministers is Yannis Varoufakis, *Adults in the Room: My Battle with Europe's Deep Establishment* (London, The Bodley Head, 2017); see also Adam Tooze, *Crashed: How a Decade of Financial Crises Changed the World* (London, Allen Lane, 2018), chapter 14.

References

Gallagher, J. and Robinson, R. "The Imperialism of Free Trade", *Economic History Review* 6, no. 1, 1953: 1–15.

Grady, J. and Grocott, C., eds. *The Continuing Imperialism of Free Trade: Developments, Trends and the Role of Supranational Agents* (London, Routledge, 2019).

Grocott, C. and Grady, J. "'Naked Abroad': The Continuing Imperialism of Free Trade", *Capital and Class* 38, no. 3, 2014: 541–562.

Harvey, D. *A Brief History of Neoliberalism* (Oxford, Oxford University Press, 2008).

Litvin, D. *Empires of Profit: Commerce, Conquest, and Corporate Responsibility* (New York, Texere, 2003).

Offer, A. and Soderberg, G. *The Nobel Factor: The Prize in Economics, Social Democracy and the Market Turn* (Princeton, New Jersey, Princeton University Press, 2016).

Robinson, R. "Non-European Foundations of European Imperialism: Sketch for a Theory of Collaboration", in Owen, R., ed. *Studies in the Theory of Imperialism* (London, Longman, 1972), 117–142.

Tooze, A. *Crashed: How a Decade of Financial Crises Changed the World* (London, Allen Lane, 2018).

Varoufakis, Y. *Adults in the Room: My Battle with Europe's Deep Establishment* (London, The Bodley Head, 2017).

9

NO SUCH THING AS SOCIETY

When Margaret Thatcher commented that 'there is no such thing as society, only individuals and families', she was channelling the convictions of the classical and neoliberal political economists.[1] As we saw in Chapter Seven, Thatcher was a convert to the work of Hayek in particular. This is no surprise; key neoliberals had been campaigning for the rejection of Keynesian ideas from as early as 1944 and had, as we saw also in Chapter Seven, formed the Mont Pèlerin Society with influential politicians and businesspeople to advance this cause.

The Conservative governments of 1979–1997 pushed for a smaller state through the sale of nationalised industries, such as train transport and gas supply, to private industry. They also undertook a refocussing of the economy away from heavy industry, such as steel production and extraction in the form of coal mining, towards a so-called entrepreneurial society. To make this happen against the strong objections of the trade union movement, the Conservative governments undertook a systematic attack on trade union organising. This took the form of physical confrontation, such as the Miner's Strike of 1984–1985, and legislative confrontation with the passing of the 1992 Trade Union and Labour Relations Act. Ultimately, the economy comprised a small but affluent financial services sector based around the City of London, and a large but poorly remunerated service sector elsewhere. Finally, the

DOI: 10.4324/9781003161950-9

Thatcher government ended decades of housebuilding by local councils and instructed councils to sell their remaining housing stock. Many of the ideas that underpinned the Conservative governments' policies could be found outlined in Friedman's *Capitalism and Freedom* as we saw in Chapter Seven. In addition, the belief of mainstream economics that there was a natural rate of unemployment called into question the need for states to take Keynesian measures to achieve full employment, allowing governments to abandon ideas of full employment. But at the same time as conceding a natural rate of unemployment, Conservative governments cast the unemployed as work-shy. By the late 1990s, public infrastructure, for example hospitals and schools, was in a dire state. And whilst privatisation of public utilities had generated substantial profits and dividends to shareholders, inequality – particularly the gap between the richest and poorest – had widened dramatically. We examine here the dismantling of social democracy and the discrediting of the ideas that underpinned it in favour of a market-based vision of the economy and society.

Neoliberalism Comes to Power

Whilst, during the 30 years since the Second World War neoliberal ideas had been implemented forcibly in countries around the world, as we saw in Chapter Eight, they had not enjoyed much popularity in Britain. This was hardly surprising. Social democracy was popular. It was based around a vision of society working together to transfer risk across generations, with those in work paying for the care of the elderly and the education of the young who, in time, would support future generations. Redistributive tax systems meant that inequality narrowed in the 30 years after the Second World War.

But, as we saw in Chapter Seven, by the end of the 1970s, three problems provided the space in which the political right could advocate for the application of neoliberal economic policies. These were, first, stagflation; second, a perception by some that trade unions had become too 'powerful'; and third, the state's ownership of a number of struggling nationalised industries. In tackling these three issues, the Thatcher government of 1979–1990 and the subsequent government of John Major, which came to an end in 1997, took the opportunity to dismantle much of the post-war social democratic state. As Tony Benn used to remark, Thatcher was not only a politician but a 'teacher'. And the message of the lesson, echoing the ideas of the classical liberals, was that individualism would lead to greater prosperity for all.

The first thing that Thatcher's government set out to do was to lower inflation in the UK through applying Friedman's ideas on monetarism to the economy. Friedman argued that it was Keynesian economic policies which had caused high inflation in both the UK and the US. The argument ran that by pumping money into the economy, governments had set up a long-term bubble of inflation which, by the 1970s, needed to be burst. Worse still, government spending and high taxes had focussed investment on the struggling nationalised industries, crowding out private investment and preventing the market from coming back to an efficient equilibrium.[2] To try to combat this, the Thatcher government set about reducing taxes on business and wealthy individuals (on the assumption that it would free up money for private investment), at the same time as working towards a balanced budget which would reduce government spending and act to gradually bring down inflation.

As Keynes could have predicted, two things would need to happen for a reduction in state spending to work on lowering inflation. First, the shrinking of government spending would cause a recession and high unemployment which would act to reduce inflation. Second, in the short term, wage levels would have to adjust quickly to operate at market levels. Keynes had argued that the second of these things was difficult because wages are sticky. Thatcher's argument was that sticky wages in 1970s and early-1980s Britain were being caused by trade unions' bargaining power which inflated the price for labour above its real market value. The breaking of this power we will come to in a bit. But, in balancing its budget and lowering taxes, what the Thatcher government had done, in effect, was to reassert the 'Treasury View' of the interwar period. The economic ideas the Thatcher government imposed would not have looked out of place to the classical liberals.

In addition to working on a balanced budget, the Conservative government spiked interest rates up to 17%. The two combined created significant unemployment. By 1982, unemployment stood at 12% of the British workforce, a level not seen since before the Second World War and double what the rate was when the Conservatives ran election campaign posters with the slogan 'Labour isn't Working'. Little wonder that comparisons between the 1930s and the 1980s have been made. Had it not been for victory in the Falklands War of 1982, the Thatcher government's dreadful economic performance could well have handed the 1983 election to the Labour Party. As it was, Thatcher was re-elected with a 144-seat majority, a significant landslide. Monetarism was abandoned by the Thatcher government by 1984, but the unemployment that it had brought with it was useful in another of Thatcher's policies – reducing the power of trade unions in the relationship between the state, business, and workers.

The 1984–1985 Miners' Strike

Jack Jones, as General Secretary of the Transport and General Workers' Union (TGWU), might well have been dubbed 'the most powerful man in Britain'. But in terms of industrial leverage, it was the National Union of Mineworkers (NUM) who led the trade union movement. In response to falling real wages in the 1960s and early 1970s, the NUM went on strike for a substantial pay rise in 1972. Staged in January and February 1972, the strike took advantage of a cold snap that put considerable pressure on power and coal supplies in the country. Forced to concede, the government offered an increase in wages of over 20%. Two years later, the NUM called for an increase in wages of 35% as inflation had eroded the gains made two years earlier. In the run-up to the announcement of the strike, which came in January 1974, the government decided to try to extend its supply of coal by implementing a three-day week. This restricted commercial electricity usage to three days a week, with further legislation restricting the broadcasting of television to no later than 10:30 at night. In scenes reminiscent of the 2020–2021 Covid lockdowns, most pubs were forced to close. The Prime Minister, Ted Heath, called a general election, asking 'Who runs Britain?' Heath hoped that the public would back the government against the miners. Instead, Heath's government fell, ushering in a minority Labour government that managed to obtain a slim majority in another general election later that year.

Thatcher had been the Education Secretary in the Heath government, famously abolishing free school milk for the over-sevens (earning her the nickname 'the milk snatcher'). Having lost her seat in the cabinet at the hands of the miners, it was little surprise that it was the NUM that Thatcher first targeted in an attempt to weaken the trade union movement. Learning from both 1972 and 1974, Thatcher's government stockpiled significant amounts of coal. Timing was important too. The National Coal Board announced the closure of 20 pits in March 1984, allowing plenty of time for a dispute to play out in the warmer summer months.

Neoliberal ideas had been forced on countries such as those of the Southern Cone by use of military dictatorship. Thatcher was certainly prepared to use levels of force against the miners, mobilising police forces from around the country to police picket lines and attempt to minimise disruption of allied industries through secondary picketing. The security services monitored the communications of NUM officials, and folklore has it that troops were provided with police uniforms and used on picket lines. The military was certainly kept on standby, with contingency plans to mobilise should the need arise. At a picket held in June 1984 at the British Steel coking plant at Orgreave, mounted police used cavalry-like charges against pickets in what became known as the Battle of Orgreave. Civil liberties were restricted, with miners travelling the country to attend pickets elsewhere being stopped by police and held stationary on motorways (secondary picketing is now unlawful but was not at the time).

The General Secretary of the NUM, Arthur Scargill, claimed that the 20 closures announced in March 1984 were the tip of the iceberg. He estimated that the government had plans to close around 70 mines. In documents released 30 years later, Scargill was proven to be correct.[3] Regardless of the signalling from the government at the time, this was clearly a battle for the future of the coal mining industry in Britain. In 1971, there were 292 pits in Britain; by 1992 only 15 remained, all of which were privatised and bought up by RJB Mining, later UK Coal. By 2020, no deep pit mining remained in Britain.

At the time, the government argued that mine closures were due to lack of profitability (a line which, as we have seen, the Conservatives had been peddling for some time in regard to nationalised industries); the desire to move away from heavy industry and into an 'entrepreneurial society'; and the supposedly poor quality of British coal (which was utterly untrue). But in the end, it was not economic facts about the future of an industry that led to the miners' strike of 1984–1985. Rather it was the desire to put free market economics ahead of social democratic ideas that was crucial. The Conservative government themselves were mining – in their case, the rich seam of neoliberal ideas that had been laid by public economists such as Hayek and Friedman in the decades before the 1980s. The ideas that nationalised industry was inefficient and that wealth lay in entrepreneurship were crucial in gaining support for the government during the 1980s. As was the idea that trade unions had too much power over the free market. The government's ability to draw upon that economic respectability allowed them to peddle a fundamental shift in how people saw themselves and their role in society. For example, during the 1983 general election, Labour's manifesto contained policies heavily inspired by social democratic ideas. But the ground was shifting so rapidly that one of Labour's own MPs, Gerald Kaufman, described the manifesto as 'the longest suicide note in history'. The description stuck, and the manifesto was then further mobilised in the right-wing press to delegitimise advocates of Keynesian and social democratic ideas.

In the end, the miners' strike was a prime example of a neoliberal intervention in the economy. In the name of a small state with low expenditures and balanced budgets, the Thatcher government spent around £7 billion on prosecuting the closures. The cost reflected the length of the strike, which ran from March 1984 to March 1985. The miners' strike was not to be the last big push of resistance that the Thatcher government faced from organised labour. Still, one by one, most of the nationalised industries were privatised during the 1980s and 1990s. Alongside this, trade union legislation was introduced to reduce the legal powers of trade unions, as we will see in Chapter Twelve.

Privatisation and Deregulation

Neoliberal ideas came into the political mainstream in the 1980s, and became dominant over Keynes' ideas in academic economics. They have remained so since, though politically they have morphed into economic austerity, as we will see in Chapter Twelve. The Thatcher government argued that where monopolies existed, they should be private ones, much as Friedman had as we saw in Chapter Seven. For supporters of nationalised industries, it did not help that a number of them were unprofitable. As we saw in Chapter Six, this was because in several cases previous governments had attempted, through nationalisations, to avoid high (albeit localised) unemployment where substantial industries were threatened. But 'the problem with socialism', Thatcher once declared, 'is that eventually you run out of other people's money.'[4] The message was clear – individuals were paying dearly to support the lost causes of others.

The Thatcher government's privatisations were extensive: British Aerospace (in two tranches, 1981 and 1985); British Airways (1987);

British Gas (1986); British Steel (1988); Rover Group (1988); National Express (1988); and the Trustee Savings Bank (TSB) (1985). In addition, from 1988 onwards, municipal bus companies were privatised. British Telecom was sold off in three tranches, in 1984, 1991, and 1993. Ironically, the initial privatisation was so profitable for the new company's shareholders that, in 1987, it provoked a strike as workers demanded their share of the profits. The strike was successful, not least because it nearly brought communications at the London Stock Exchange to its knees. However, one of the longer-term effects of the strike was that the huge backlog of work which the strike had caused damaged BT's reputation, providing justifications to downgrade the terms and conditions of the company's workers in the name of efficiency.

Whilst it is Thatcher who springs to mind as the nemesis of the miners, it was in fact John Major's government that privatised British Coal in 1994. Prior to that, the Central Electricity Generating Board was privatised in 1991 and National Power and PowerGen were formed as new private companies which took ownership of coal-fired power stations. The last stage in the process of privatising electricity production was the sale of nuclear power generation in 1995. After that, they were bought, sold, and merged, forming what are now the 'big five' energy companies. Major also privatised Scottish Hydro-Electric (1991); the Severn Bridge (1992); the Stationery Office (part of HMSO) (1996); and, particularly controversially, British Rail (1994–1997). By the time the Conservative governments were finished, nearly all the public monopolies were in the hands of private oligopolies.

In theory, the creation of a private oligopoly out of a public monopoly implies that the state achieved its objective of bringing competition to public services and with it the benefits of competition in a free market. Friedman had argued that private monopolies were usually preferable because they at least opened up the possibility of new entrants to the market. But in reality, many of these services remain monopolies. Take, for example, train companies. Whilst there are a variety of these, you can only take one operator's service from Leicester to Birmingham. In terms of value for money, prices increase annually at an extraordinary rate. Every January, prices increase by the level of inflation according to the Retail Price Index (a widely discredited measure of inflation that just so happens to be higher than the more reliable Consumer Price Index) plus 1% on designated commuter routes. The fares on non-commuter routes are unregulated. And commuters who find themselves crammed into old carriages of which there aren't enough might think that the long-lamented British Rail cheese sandwich is a small price to pay for a non-profit alternative. Franchises can be bought and sold, but genuine competition can't happen because, despite Friedman's reasoning, the cost of laying new track is too prohibitive.

To stay a little longer with the example of the rail network, one of the side effects of privatisation has been the need for state subsidies of privatised public services. This is because many of the routes are considered unprofitable for private business. In other parts of the rail infrastructure, the performance of the private sector was so poor that subsequent governments were forced to renationalise it. In 2002, Railtrack was taken back into government control, in part as an outcome of the initial enquiry into the Hatfield train crash. The crash occurred in 2000, when a train travelling between London and Leeds was derailed in the Hatfield area by cracks in the rails that caused them to eventually fail under the weight of the train. Four passengers were killed. Part of the problem was that skilled former British Rail engineers had left Railtrack and been replaced by cheaper, less skilled staff.[5] In addition, unlike in Germany where social democratic ideas of board management still have influence, there is no requirement ensuring worker representation on boards in the UK, leaving boards bereft of the technical knowledge held by their staff.

The creation of Network Rail out of Railtrack had only been a part-nationalisation as the newly formed company was still contracting out large parts of its operations. This outsourcing was identified as a major cause of the Potters Bar train crash of 2002. The crash occurred when a train going from King's Cross to King's Lynn was partially derailed by a faulting set of points, causing the rear of the train to collide with the Potters Bar train station, coming to rest on the platform. Seven died, and over 70 were injured. The resulting investigation blamed poor maintenance by the private contractor, Jarvis PLC, for the problem with the points, but it also exposed broader concerns about just how seriously private contractors were taking health and safety.

So much for the innate efficiency of private enterprise. Nevertheless, the sale of the nationalised industries to private enterprise was very profitable. Invariably, on the eve of privatisation, a nationalised company had its assets transferred to a company that was then floated on the stock market. Given that many of the privatised companies were sitting on monopolies, the share prices tended to shoot up on the day of the sale. Or, we would argue, time and again the assets were sold off too cheaply, and not just by the Conservative governments of the 1980s and 1990s. In 2013, the then coalition government of Conservatives and Liberal Democrats privatised Royal Mail, which had been a state-owned company for nearly 500 years. On the first day, the share price rose 38%, representing a massive return on investment in one day alone for those in big finance who had access to the initial share issue.[6]

A crucial part of making Royal Mail an attractive offering for investors was the government's decision to take on responsibility for the Royal Mail pension scheme, which was in deficit to the tune of around £10 billion. Since then, the deficit has worsened considerably. Worse still, because of the coalition government's obsession with balancing its budgets, the government sold off most of the assets which the scheme had and paid off government debt with it. In other words, the government got a temporary boon but future generations of taxpayers will have to cover the costs of the scheme. Much like the example of subsidised rail franchises, neoliberal ideas have increased the size and cost of the state as a result of policies supposedly meant to reduce it.

The reaction of many to the underpriced sale of Royal Mail was one of resignation to a government that seemed intent on rewarding financial elites (though no doubt it was one of glee for those high-level investors who got in on the original share option). In the early days of privatisation, however, things were different. The government was working against a backdrop of accepted national ownership of key industries. We have seen one way in which the government persuaded people that nationalised industries should be privatised, and that was through the idea that those industries were inherently inefficient and that, in keeping with Friedman, the existence of merely the possibility of competition would lead to more efficient, and therefore cheaper, services for people. But another was the government's marketing of the sales as being part of creating a 'shareholder democracy'.

As Amy Edwards has extensively demonstrated, the deregulation of the City of London's stock market and investment industry opened the way for more individuals to invest in shares for the first time.[7] Some were knowledgeable enough to invest for themselves. Others joined investment clubs, feeling their way through the market with other eager investors. A range of products became available, not just investments in one company, but packages of investments designed to reduce risk and be more likely to return a profit. The Conservative government used this to sell the idea that the public could profit from their ownership of utilities as shareholders, rather than lose money to 'failing' nationalised industries as taxpayers. The adverts for the sale of shares, such as the 'Tell Sid' adverts that accompanied the privatisation of British Gas, were selling not just a product but also a change in ideas of how people should think about the provision of utilities. Yet, whilst it is true that the number of people who had investments in shares increased dramatically in the 1980s and beyond, in reality, the majority of those shares found their way to big business such as pensions funds and investment banks.

'No Such Thing as Society'

As we saw in Chapter Six, by the end of the 1970s, just below one-third of housing in Britain was council owned or in the hands of housing associations. Council housing had served two main purposes since the first council housing Act in 1919. First, it was designed to provide decent housing to the general population. Much of the private housing of inner cities was at this time slum housing. Some of this housing was particularly appalling – homes with no windows, or 'back-to-back' housing, essentially a one-up, one-down house, the rear wall of which was the rear wall of another property attached at the back. And whilst this post-First World War housing was prompted to some extent by loftier goals – 'homes fit for heroes' as the wartime Prime Minister David Lloyd George had called for – the second reason for council housing was that army recruiters believed that the poor health of British conscripts during the war owed much to poor housing conditions.

The well-intentioned planning that went into council house builds was considerable. Interwar housing tended to provide a good amount of space in semi-detached houses that also came with a garden area large enough for some subsistence gardening to take. People who had previously lived in slums, such as the residents of newly built Wythenshawe, first built in the 1920s and vastly expanded after the Second World War, found themselves on spacious, cherry tree-lined boulevards and crescents that were covered in pink blossom in the spring. After the war, many developments went upwards in the hope of creating cities in the sky. Park Hill housing estate in Sheffield was at the cutting edge of architectural science and art. First built at the end of the 1950s and finished in the early 1960s, it replaced back-to-back housing on the site.

Walkways and staircases linked high-rise buildings together without the need to go down to ground level to walk between individual buildings. Experiments such as the design of Milton Keynes were enthusiastically taken up. There, traffic and pedestrians were kept separate through a system of bridges and underpasses meaning that the two need never meet. Roundabouts became the vogue, the idea being that traffic would flow organically, rather than stop-start as at conventional crossroads with traffic lights.

But by the end of the 1970s, there was considerable criticism to level at these developments. The high-rise developments soon became the focus of antisocial behaviours. Staircases and walkways intended to bond communities together became rat-runs for criminals. Faulty lifts posed perennial problems for the disabled and elderly. Communal spaces, the care of which seemed to be the responsibility of nobody, became dilapidated and were poorly lit. Rather than a city in the sky, people found themselves relocated to a concrete jungle. It didn't help that the commonly used brutalist architecture had a habit of looking like something from the Soviet Union, itself in chronic decline by the 1980s. In Manchester and Sheffield, grey concrete buildings stood, depressingly, against the backdrop of a grey sky.

Elsewhere, in Glasgow, the local corporation undertook a series of slum clearances from the 1930s onwards. To achieve the scale required, the corporation moved around 250,000 people from the city centre to four peripheral housing estates. The estates were of considerably better quality in comparison with the slums where people were moved from. But poor design meant that the housing became dilapidated quickly. Worse still, moved from inner-city areas, people struggled to commute to jobs, and jobs on the estates were few. Families and communities that were once close together were dispersed, causing unhappiness. Lack of facilities led to antisocial behaviour, and lack of jobs created gang violence. Even the English low-rise semi-detached buildings were not universally welcome. In some developments, council planners took care to place houses in such a way as to not overlook each other, to offer privacy unknown in slum dwellings such as back-to-backs. But the relocation to new estates dis-located people from their former communities, and the private nature of the new estates made making new ones a struggle. Reminiscing fondly about slum housing was a dire judgement on the new developments.

As with the crises of unemployment and inflation, in the failures of council housing Thatcher found an opportunity to effect a sea-change in ideas around council housing. Whilst it is true that both Conservative and Labour governments had for decades before the 1980s seen private home ownership as a goal to be striven for, they still saw council provision as an important safety net. But in keeping with Friedman's idea that state support for those suffering hardship was in fact an invitation to welfare dependency, Thatcher cast council housing as something that was encouraging people to live on benefits. As she put it in an interview with *Women's Own* in 1987:

> 'I am homeless, the Government must house me!' and so they are casting their problems on society... It is our duty to look after ourselves... somehow there are some people who have been manipulating the system... when people come and say: 'But what is the point of working? I can get as much on the dole!'[8]

That it was an individual's responsibility to house themselves was underscored again in 2023 when the then Home Secretary Suella Braverman claimed that homelessness was a lifestyle choice.[9]

In order to reduce the amount of council housing available, the government passed the Housing Act (1980) which gave six million people the 'right to buy' their council house, of which about one-third actually did so. Tenants were given a discount on the price of their property as well as deposit-free mortgages from their council. Over two million people have since bought their homes through the scheme. However, as we will soon see, there was to be a serious growth in the price of housing from the 1980s onwards. Those who could afford to buy tended to make large profits when selling their properties. Those who couldn't found that they had missed the boat when it came to buying a property and, of course, for those worst off, the available stock of council-provided housing dwindled. Many of the houses bought under the scheme eventually found themselves bought up by private landlords.[10]

You might have thought that all of these houses entering the private housing market would have acted to reduce house prices by increasing demand but it didn't. First of all, there was a minimum period after the purchase of a council house during which owners were not allowed to sell their properties on. And, of course, not everyone sold straight away when the period ended, resulting in a drip-drip of properties onto the market. It was actually a development elsewhere, as part of the Thatcher government's deregulation of the finance industry, that sparked a growth in house prices. Before 1986, only building societies were allowed to offer mortgages but the Building Societies Act (1986) now allowed banks to offer mortgages. This was significant because the two funded their mortgages very differently. Building societies could only lend money for mortgages out of their deposits, in other words out of the money on deposit with them. This gave house prices an indirect link to wages because the money available for buying a house came from the savings people were making from their income. By contrast, banks simply create a mortgage account for you and deposit in it your debt. But it isn't real money, it is simply made up. In this way, banks don't lend you other people's money to buy your house, they simply create the money out of thin air. What this also means is that when you pay off your mortgage, you are actually destroying the money created rather than paying the money back.[11]

Allowing banks to give mortgages broke the link between earnings and house prices. Most building societies converted into banks. Housing was an excellent asset for banks because defaults in payments led to the banks being able to seize the house and sell it off. Buy-to-let mortgages allowed those who could raise mortgages with banks to benefit from income handed over by those who could not afford to buy. As houses became seen as assets, their worth increased. For those on lower incomes who did manage to raise a mortgage, the level of debt which they faced compared to their income increased. Handing out cheap debt for housing led to the sub-prime mortgage scandal of 2007, which brought about the financial crash of 2007–2008. As we will see in Chapter Eleven, the amount of personal debt held by individuals has been increasing with, at times, the debt only being serviced by taking out more debt.

One side effect of this boom in private ownership of housing was the creation of a swathe of people who, having previously had no real interest in them, were now embedded within financial markets. On the one hand, those with mortgages became concerned with the health of financial markets, and in particular the interest rates needed to contain or encourage them, naturally preferring low rates. On the other hand, those living off savings, often pensioners, were keen to see higher interest rates. This created a generational divide between those in work and paying mortgages, and the retired, whose financial interests were opposed to one another. Later on, as house prices rose above levels of affordability for the lower paid, the inability of many to get on the housing ladder created yet another divide between those older workers who could afford mortgages and those dubbed to be of 'generation rent' who could not, pitting generations against each other.

Conclusion

The tendency of those who follow neoliberal ideas has been to explain that any of their failures are created by neoliberalism not being implemented fully. In other words, the 'answer' to policy failures caused by neoliberal ideas, whether they come from mainstream economists or politicians, is to keep going with more of the same. Keynes had identified this problem in his letter to Hayek in which he outlined his response to *The Road to Serfdom*. Keynes' concern was that, when it came to what should be the responsibility of business and what should be the responsibility of the state, Hayek did not draw a clear line. For the political right, this has proved advantageous. Whereas Hayek spent decades trying to answer Keynes' critique, politicians have simply taken the idea that the state is inherently inefficient, perhaps even a threat to personal liberty, and pressed that point repeatedly. As a result, a defence of social democratic policies has become extremely difficult to attract voters to. The UK Labour Party found this under Jeremy Corbyn. The idea of a Green New Deal was inspired by the ideas of Keynes and of the social democracies of the post-war era. But it faced considerable opposition from the mainstream media, much of which argued that the policy would be unaffordable and would crowd out private investment. Under Keir Starmer, the Labour Party has refocussed its policies in such a way as to fit neoliberal political ideas, dramatically slashing proposed spending on green investment.

Notes

1 Margaret Thatcher, Interview for *Woman's Own*, 1987.
2 See Chapter Seven for the idea of crowding out.
3 Nick Higham, "Cabinet Papers Reveal 'Secret Coal Pits Closure Plan'", *BBC News*, 3 January 2014, https://www.bbc.co.uk/news/uk-25549596.
4 Margaret Thatcher, Interview for *This Week*, Thames TV, 5 February 1976.
5 Between 2000 and 2006 there were a series of enquiries into the crash, culminating in, "Train Derailment at Hatfield: A Final Report by the Independent Investigation Board" (London, Office of Rail Regulation, July 2006), available at https://www.railwaysarchive.co.uk/documents/HSE_Hatfield Final2006.pdf.

6 Rupert Neate, Nicholas Watt, and Larry Elliott, "Royal Mail Shares Soar 38% as Labour Complains of Knockdown Price", *The Guardian*, 11 October 2013.
7 For the development of a shareholder democracy, and an assessment of its extent, see Amy Edwards, *Are We Rich Yet? The Rise of Mass Investment Culture in Contemporary Britain* (Oakland, University of California Press, 2022).
8 Thatcher, Interview for *Woman's Own*, 1987.
9 Mark Townsend and Michael Savage, "Fury as Braverman Depicts Homelessness as a 'Lifestyle Choice'", *The Guardian*, 4 November 2023.
10 For an outline of the sale of council housing, see Daniel Stedman Jones, *Masters of the Universe: Hayek, Friedman, and the Birth of Neoliberal Politics* (Princeton, New Jersey, Princeton University Press, 2012), chapter 7.
11 For the changing regulations on mortgages, see Avner Offer, "The Market Turn: From Social Democracy to Market Liberalism", *The Economic History Review* 70, no. 4, 2017: 1051–1071.

References

"Train Derailment at Hatfield: A Final Report by the Independent Investigation Board" (London, Office of Rail Regulation, July 2006), https://www.railwaysa rchive.co.uk/documents/HSE_HatfieldFinal2006.pdf (accessed 4 April 2024).

Edwards, A. *Are We Rich Yet? The Rise of Mass Investment Culture in Contemporary Britain* (Oakland, University of California Press, 2022).

Higham, N. "Cabinet Papers Reveal 'Secret Coal Pits Closure Plan'", *BBC News*, 3 January 2014, https://www.bbc.co.uk/news/uk-25549596 (accessed 2 April 2024).

Neate, R., Watt, N., and Elliott, L. "Royal Mail Shares Soar 38% as Labour Complains of Knockdown Price", *The Guardian*, 11 October 2013.

Offer, A. "The Market Turn: From Social Democracy to Market Liberalism", *The Economic History Review* 70, no. 4, 2017: 1051–1071.

Stedman Jones, D. *Masters of the Universe: Hayek, Friedman, and the Birth of Neoliberal Politics* (Princeton, New Jersey, Princeton University Press, 2012).

Townsend, M. and Savage, M. "Fury as Braverman Depicts Homelessness as a 'Lifestyle Choice'", *The Guardian*, 4 November 2023.

10

THINGS CAN ONLY GET BETTER

In 1990, the Conservative Party toppled Margaret Thatcher as leader and elected John Major in her place. Thatcher had served economic elites well, albeit, for ordinary people, at the cost of dismantling the social democratic state. As Tony Benn put it, Thatcher's period in office had been characterised by 'tax cuts for the rich, benefit cuts for the poor'. But by 1990, Thatcher's usefulness had waned. In 1989, the introduction of the so-called Poll Tax (officially the Community Charge) led to riots. The Poll Tax replaced the previous local Rates system (which looked very much like Council Tax does these days). Instead of households paying a certain amount of money to the local council based on the value of the house in which they lived, the Poll Tax charged a flat rate per person. This meant that a family of four with two adults in a working-class household would pay double what one person in a mansion paid. In response, up and down the country there were mass protests and riots. A particularly violent scene broke out in Trafalgar Square in March 1990 which left over 100 protestors and 100 police officers injured. A mass non-payment campaign sprang up, with one in three refusing to pay. Thatcher's popularity was seriously on the wane, and the Conservatives came to realise that they were running a real risk of losing the next general election. After a couple of leadership challenges, Thatcher vowed to fight on, only to discover that her Cabinet largely refused to support her. She left office on 28 November 1990.

DOI: 10.4324/9781003161950-10

John Major tried to establish himself as a 'one nation' Conservative – the wing of the party which traditionally had some sympathy with social democratic ideas. The abolition of the Poll Tax was meant to go some way towards proving that. But as we saw in Chapter Nine, the Major government's economic policies continued along the same lines as the ideas of his predecessor. Major introduced league tables for services such as the NHS and British Rail, which, in the end, were used to hammer public services for failure to meet targets and, so, open them to the accusation that they were inefficient. Unsurprisingly, then, privatisations continued. Workers' terms and conditions were deregulated in the name of the market, with the relaxation of the laws on Sunday trading and Britain opting out of the part of the Maastricht Treaty which extended further guarantees of workers' rights, such as limiting the maximum hours in the working week. We also saw in Chapter Nine that the Major government abolished the vast majority of wages councils (the last one to be abolished was the Agricultural Workers Wage Council, which survived much longer than others, being finally abolished by the coalition government in 2013 as part of the 'bonfire of the quangos'). At the same time, the right to organise was made more difficult by the Trade Union Act 1992.

Despite the promises that came with the expansion of free market principles to nationalised industries and the labour market, alongside attempts to create the classical small state, the Major government faced economic crisis, much as the Thatcher government had. A recession in the early 1990s saw inflation go above 10% and unemployment hit around three million people. On 'Black Wednesday', 16 September 1992, Britain's currency collapsed as a result of currency speculators taking advantage of Britain's membership of the European Exchange Rate Mechanism. The hedge fund manager George Soros, for example, made $1 billion by betting against the pound on the currency markets, in the process earning himself the nickname 'the man who broke the Bank of England'. Wracked by economic crisis, alongside a series of unfortunate moral scandals that unsettled Major's 'back to basics', family-centred social policy, Major's ability to implement policy became precarious. In the 1992 general election, the Conservatives won with a slim majority of 21 seats. But as the years rolled on, by-elections, defections, and the withdrawal of the whip from Conservative MPs whittled down this majority so that, by the time of the 1997 general election, the Conservative government was a minority one.

The Rise of the Third Way

With neoliberalism in seeming crisis, the Labour Party opposition in the early 1990s could have taken the opportunity to reassert social democratic policies as an antidote to the individualistic, market-driven ideas that dominated the 18 years of Conservative rule. But the Conservative championing of neoliberal economic ideas, combined with the shift in the economy from an industrial one to a financial services, white-collar, and hospitality-based one, had changed attitudes in Britain tremendously. The Labour Party's reaction to this had been a steady move to the centre-ground from the Kinnock years onwards. For example, in 1981, the party's congress managed to change the method of leadership elections. They did away with the system whereby the party's leader was elected by the party's Members of Parliament in favour of an electoral college system. Under this, the affiliated trade unions held 40% of the votes, party members 30%, and MPs 30%. Crucially, the union vote was exercised by that union's General Secretary. So, for example, if a union had half a million members, then that would allot half a million votes to that union's preferred candidate. As a way of connecting leaders to their base, it made some sense. But giving the trade unions a large say in the process at the precise time when the Thatcher government was popularising the idea that unions were the problem in the British economy gave the Conservatives a massive stick with which to beat Labour over the head.

The system changed in some measure in 1993 when the rules were, by a narrow margin, changed. In the new system, the unions had one-third of the votes, members one-third, and MPs one-third. But the union vote was to be exercised by union members. Under this system, if our example trade union of half a million members only had 10,000 members take part in the vote, then that was all their candidate could get, and of course, those votes could also be spread amongst the candidates. There were also other qualifications, such as having to have a certain number of nominations from within the party's MPs. The significance of this change was hotly contested, but it did herald in the New Labour era under the leaderships of Tony Blair, Gordon Brown (who had so many nominations from MPs that a leadership election was not triggered), and (out of government) Ed Miliband.

From 1994 until 2010, under the leaderships of Tony Blair and then Gordon Brown, the Labour Party styled itself New Labour. Apart from the changes to the leadership election, internal party reforms reflected the broader neoliberal economic landscape. The party rewrote Clause IV of its constitution. This had previously set out a policy of using the state to nationalise industry in such a way as to give workers ownership of, to use Marx's phrase, 'the means of production'. In effect, it was Clause IV that made the Labour party a socialist one. New Labour rejected this in favour of a market-based economy, albeit with some public ownership. The idea, first laid out by the sociologist Anthony Giddens, was that New Labour would forge a 'third way' between capitalism and socialism.[1]

The third way was a commitment that Labour would not return to pre-Thatcher social democratic ideas. The renationalisation of public utilities was ruled out, guaranteeing the interests of the large multinational companies that had bought up, for a song, Britain's infrastructure and which are still making massive profits, despite clear failings (a good example being the ailing water supply and waste water disposal problems faced, in particular, since 2020).[2] At the same time, New Labour was committed to neoliberalism's idea that trade union power would throw the market out of equilibrium and create inefficiency. No attempt was made to positively reform the 1992 Trade Union Act. The New Labour government even tried to tempt employers to Britain by boasting that Britain had trade union legislation that favoured employers more than in most continental European countries. As Blair put it in his 1997 election campaign, 'the changes that we propose [to trade union laws] would leave British law the most restrictive on trade unions in the western world.'[3]

The ideas that neoliberals had used to subvert social democracy had become so dominant by the mid-1990s that it was impossible for opposition parties to frame their policies in terms of social democratic ideas. Not, perhaps, that they wanted to. As Peter Mandelson, New Labour's infamous spin doctor, put it, New Labour was 'intensely relaxed about people getting filthy rich as long as they pay their taxes'.[4] The change of tack worked. During the 1997 election campaign, the *Sun* newspaper, ironically a better barometer of the attitudes of elites than of ordinary people, came out in support of New Labour. But if neoliberalism in power had been about finding new markets for business to move into through privatisation, the New Labour government was faced with something of a problem. By 1997 there were not many nationalised industries left to privatise. Certainly, the largest ones had already been bought up during the Thatcher and Major eras. There was also another problem which New Labour needed to face in order to maintain its electoral base. By the mid- to late 1990s, public infrastructure was in a terrible state. Many state-school-educated people who went to school during this time will remember being taught in Portakabins due to overcrowding in classrooms.

The answer to both problems came in the massive increase in the use of Private Finance Initiatives (PFIs) to replace ailing infrastructure. Private firms were invited to tender for all sorts of building work, including schools, university halls, hospitals, libraries, and the like. The firms would put up the money for building the asset, whilst the user, say, a hospital trust, would pay rent for a period, perhaps 20 or 30 years. The risks to the companies who won PFI contracts were minimal as the debt they raised to carry out the initial project work was underwritten by the government. Staff who would previously have been employed by the state, for example cleaners in hospitals, were often transferred to private companies on worse terms and conditions (particularly in relation to pensions).

The Gambling Industry and the Ideas That Rule Us

There were some 'ordinary' privatisations under New Labour: student loan portfolios and British nuclear fuels, for example. More importantly, the third way finished the process of introducing the private sector into traditionally state-run public sector services. PFI put capital projects into the hands of the private sector, whilst contracting out, itself a vision of the so-called efficiency of the market, saw the private sector invited into schools (for example in catering) and the National Health Service (to the extent that it is debatable whether or not we can actually say that the NHS is state-owned). In the finance sector, lax regulation and weak enforcement set up the conditions which led to the financial crisis of 2007–2008, as we will see in Chapter Eleven. Free market, small-state ideas began to dictate not only the way in which the economy operates, but also how the responsibilities of the state have altered to accommodate this. A particularly good case study lies in reform of the gambling industry, from the mid-2000s, with the 2005 Gambling Act.

Whilst gambling in Britain had been legal, if heavily restricted, since the mid-nineteenth century, it was only in the latter part of the twentieth century that significant reform was introduced. In 1960, gambling that took place away from the trackside (of horse and greyhound races) was legalised, allowing bookies in the community to apply for licenses to legally take bets. Later in the 1960s, legislation was brought in to regulate gambling in casinos and clubs, which, the government felt, could not be regulated by the existing legislation on betting and gaming. This helped to allay fears that gambling had become 'mafialike'. Licensing and policy were held by the Home Office (responsible for policing and crime). Further reforms were introduced as part of the outcome of the report of the Royal Commission of 1978 chaired by Lord Rothschild.

Gambling legislation from the 1960s until the 2005 Gambling Act, broadly, reflected social democratic principles. On the one hand, there was a recognition that here was a service that people wanted to use and which companies wanted to supply. On the other hand, there was a sense that the government needed to protect people from harm arising from gambling addiction and crime associated with the industry. Outside of the trackside bookies, to get a license to set up a bookmakers required applicants to demonstrate demand for the shop to a Magistrates' Court. By not allowing bookmakers to try to create demand, but only follow it, licenses could be restricted, which helped from the point of view of policing and also kept faith groups onside (religious organisations often make strong, and critical, contributions to enquiries on gambling reform). Advertising was banned, and bookies' premises were to be discreet (anyone watching the Premier League in 2023–2024, with three teams sponsored by betting companies, knows where this story of deregulation is going...).

In 1999, five years after the introduction of the National Lottery, the first country-wide lottery in Britain's history, and not long after New Labour's election, the government commissioned Sir Alan Budd to undertake a review of the gambling industry. Whereas Rothschild's report had been a Royal Commission, established through the Home Office, Budd's report was commissioned by the Department for Culture, Media, and Sport (DCMS). Rothschild was an aristocrat, biologist, and policy advisor to various governments who, in the 1980s, joined the Rothschild family bank. Budd was Chief Economic Advisor to the Treasury during the Major years. Whereas the spirit of Rothschild's report was that the status quo was a good starting point, Budd's report led Tessa Jowell, Secretary of State at DCMS, to write in her foreword to the government's response to the report that, 'modernisation of our gambling laws is long overdue.'[5]

The Budd report was published in 2001, the same time that responsibility for gambling was moved from the Home Office to DCMS, a symbolic rethinking of what kind of activity gambling was. The report put at its heart the idea that the individual's economic freedom to spend their money how they wished should be central to gambling reform. This was explicitly put; 'the state should respect the right of the individual to behave as he or she wishes.'[6] In the following government consultation on legal reform, the stated aim of new legislation was to 'remove unnecessary barriers to customer access to gambling'. To achieve this, the need to demonstrate unmet demand; strict regulations on where in the country casinos could be located; the need to have a 'cooling off' period of 24 hours between signing up for a casino or bingo hall and playing; the ban on advertising gambling products; the ban on using credit cards for lottery tickets or scratch cards; and protection for gamblers from the courts being used to retrieve gambling debts, were all abolished. Free market appeals were easy to justify, mainly because of the National Lottery. The government argued that 90% of people had gambled within the year before 2001, but it should be noted that 73% of those people played the lottery and 58% had bought a raffle ticket. Only 15% had bet on the horses or greyhounds, and only 13% on gaming machines.[7]

In the early 2000s, the country saw a change in emphasis on the balance between the state and the individual's responsibility to prevent harm to gamblers. In addition, a long-running dispute between bookmakers and casinos over gaming machines was lurking in the background of the consultation and the new legislation on gambling. Before the 2005 Gambling Act, the law had been clear that games of chance such as roulette could only be played in casinos. In 1999, gaming machines that allowed people to play casino games in bookmakers (and we're largely talking roulette here) were introduced and, after a tax break on games that return smaller margins to the operator was introduced, these proliferated from 2001 onwards. Technically, so the casinos argued, these were illegal because only casinos were allowed to operate games of chance in the UK. However, the bookmakers pointed out that the actual 'spin of the wheel' did not take place in the UK, rather in offshore territories that did not have laws restricting roulette to casinos, with the outcome merely being reported to the betting terminal in the bookies. An uneasy truce broke out between the book-makers and the casinos. Neither wanted to get into a court to prove whether or not bookies had the legal right to operate these gaming machines in case they lost. Instead, both sides agreed that bookmakers would limit the number of machines in each shop to a maximum of four. But after successful lobbying by the bookmakers, the 2005 Gambling Act finally legalised these machines.

The limit of four machines per bookmaker's shop explains why, from 2005 until 2019 (when they were, for practical purposes, abolished, as we will see), it was not uncommon to see two branches of, say, Lad-brokes next to each other on the high street. Very quickly from 2005, gaming machines (more technically known as Fixed Odds Betting Terminals) proliferated. They were extremely profitable because, whilst the return on them was small, it was guaranteed at a level of around 2.7%. But for gamblers, these machines could swallow enormous sums of money. The maximum stake was £100, with a quick play button allowing three bets per minute, allowing someone to stake £18,000 an hour. At the peak, there were around 33,000 Fixed Odds Betting Terminals in Britain, with a greater density of them in more deprived areas, and a turnover of around £40 billion.[8] The 2005 Act not only proliferated the number of betting shops in which Fixed Odds Betting Terminals could be placed, but also extended their opening hours, allowing them to open from 8am until 10pm. And in them, Fixed Odds Betting Terminal bets exceeded traditional over-the-counter bets on things likes the dogs and horse races. It was big money, and as often happens when big money moves into an industry, smaller independent bookies were practically wiped out. More importantly, though, an extraordinary amount of problem gambling, and organised crime, followed in their wake.

Quite how many people were problematic gamblers and regularly played Fixed Odds Betting Terminals will probably never be known. This is because self-identification is difficult. In 2017, a Gambling Commission report estimated that two million people were either struggling with gambling addictions, or at risk of one, of which a sig-nificant amount was linked to Fixed Odd Betting Terminals.[9] Because self-identification is difficult, targeting low-level intervention strategies is difficult. As the 2005 Act placed the responsibility for coping with pro-blem gambling largely on individuals, the main protection from gam-bling was self-exclusion from a bookmaker's premises. The problem was, of course, that there were simply so many bookies that self-exclusion wasn't much of a barrier to a relapse.

Fixed Odds Betting Terminals also became associated with targeting deprived areas and organised crime. For example, in 2012 the 50 parliamentary constituencies that had the highest unemployment gambled collectively £5.6 billion, whilst the 50 lowest-unemployment constituencies gambled about one-quarter of that, £1.4 billion. It was certainly the case that there were more terminals in more deprived areas. When the Conservative MP John Redwood was asked why less affluent areas had more Fixed Odds Betting Terminals, his response was, 'I put it down to the fact that poor people believe there's one shot to get rich. They put getting rich down to luck and think they can take a gamble. They also have time on their hands. My voters are too busy working hard to make a reasonable home.'[10] Rich stuff indeed coming from a man who made his money as an investment manager.

Redwood's reaction to the issues surrounding Fixed Odds Betting Terminals sums up nicely many of the themes we have seen throughout this book. The idea that those in more deprived areas are feckless with their money, contrasted against the hard work of others, can be used to justify cutting social security provision. In fact, the 2005 Gambling Act was worded in such a way as to imply that investments in the stock exchange could be considered as gambling and so should be regulated by the Gaming Commission. This required an investigation and amendments to legislation to be introduced to prevent this. Ultimately, gambling on the horses or on the stock market aren't too far apart from each other.

It was not just problem gambling that came with the legalisation of the Fixed Odds Betting Terminals, but also issues involving organised crime. The problem that very successful criminals who deal in cash have faced since the time of Al Capone is what to do with all the cash you have but aren't supposed to. It can hardly be banked, and spending it in any way that is traceable would, upon investigation, reveal a very suspicious gap between spendings and tax paid on income. But Fixed Odds Betting Terminals were ideal in these situations. Drug dealers could take their cash into a bookies and sit themselves down at a Fixed Odds Betting Terminal. By betting, say, £20 on black and £20 on red, with £2 on the green zero, the most they could lose was the £2 on green. Or, if green comes out, then they win £72 less the £40 on the red and black. After a while, they could cash out, getting a receipt and, to all appearances, be holding onto legal gambling winnings rather than drug money. It was because of their addictiveness that Fixed Odds Betting Terminals were called 'the crack cocaine of gambling', but the irony of likening them to a drug when they were used to clean money from the drug trade was grim.

Almost from the moment the 2005 Gambling Act legalised Fixed Odds Betting Terminals, campaign groups argued that the machines should be banned on grounds of the problem gambling and organised crime that became associated with them. After a very long-running battle, the machines were, effectively, banned when, in 2019, the maximum stake was reduced from £100 to £2. Almost overnight thousands of bookies closed; after all, they weren't there for bets on the races or horses, but for the Fixed Odds Betting Terminals. That it took 14 years for the campaign against Fixed Odds Betting Terminals to succeed was largely due to the persistence of the betting companies. For a start, they are extremely resistant to allowing research on gambling which has not been commissioned or funded by themselves to take place. The result of this is that much of the research on gambling is ambiguous as to the extent of problem gambling. When research does investigate the causes of problem gambling, it often focusses on a 'failure' on the part of the individual. For example, some studies suggest that problem gambling occurs more commonly amongst those who have or who have recovered from drug addiction. Others suggest those in the neurodivergent population, such as autistic people, are more prone to problem gambling.[11] Little research focusses on the idea that the state should make industry-wide interventions to protect gamblers from harm.

Bookies were also good at organising lobbying campaigns against attempts to ban Fixed Odds Betting Terminals. One such attempt took place in 2012, prompting the industry to launch its 'Back Your Local Bookie' campaign – something of an irony, given that the big betting companies have all but wiped out true local bookies. The language used reveals the seeming common sense of the right of the individual to economic freedom. A petition against the banning of Fixed Odds Betting Terminals read, 'I should be able to spend time and money there if I choose, and I don't support government action that threatens to take away that freedom.' The petition went on with a veiled threat: 'and also puts jobs at risk'.[12] Given that bookies were disproportionately located in deprived areas, threatening a big jump in unemployment (a total of around 10,000) in those areas was a serious threat.

In the end, it's hard to imagine that the betting industry simply gave up on Fixed Odds Betting Terminals (and, given their campaigning, harder still to believe they were convinced to prevent harm from coming to problem gamblers). Instead, the 2005 Gambling Act, unknowingly, opened the way for technology to present more effective ways of encouraging gambling. Despite the industry's best efforts, bookies were still off-putting to many people, in particular women. But the development of apps that people could download to their phones negated the need for such a large, fixed estate of bookmakers' shops and allowed for a more welcoming presentation. In addition to casino games and betting on sport, even games of bingo can now be played online. Lifting the ban on advertising meant that, in the 2023–2024 Premier League season, three teams played in front of large crowds, with an even larger number of watchers online and on programmes such as Match of the Day, wearing advertising of gambling companies on their shirts as sponsorship. Of course, there are concerns and calls for regulation of the relationship between betting and sport and of the apps on which people bet, but the 2005 Gambling Act could not have even dreamed of such a development, let alone regulated it well. For now, bookies are back to having a large portion of their income only very lightly regulated.

The story of Fixed Odds Betting Terminals is wrapped up in the extension of the market throughout the economy and the retreat of regulation even in areas where, traditionally, it was. Deregulation had catastrophic effects for everyone when the 2007–2008 crash hit (see Chapter Eleven), but deregulation in gambling specifically has certainly had dire effects for a good number of people too. In the New Labour era, much was made of 'modernising' and 'efficiency', which were largely euphemisms for reducing democratic control and opening up organisations and industries, such as universities and gambling, to the market. But not every country followed this path. In Norway, for example, money from North Sea oil extraction was used to create a sovereign wealth fund which now underpins Norway's social security system. And in its gambling industry, heavy regulation helps greatly to prevent harm from problem gambling. There, gambling is offered only by two state-run companies, with limits on how much players can bet.

Conclusion

New Labour came to power in 1997 on a platform to rejuvenate the UK economy, but had to do so in a way that would not bring back visions of the economic problems of the 1970s. To do this it turned to the idea of the 'third way'. Designed to be an alternative pathway between capitalism and socialism, New Labour nevertheless embraced the reliance on markets which the previous Conservative governments had introduced. This meant that the remaining nationalised industries were largely sold off. Public infrastructure did receive investment, but only as part of PFIs, where upfront investment from firms into the public sector was rewarded by lease-back arrangements with lengthy contracts. This was justified on the basis that self-interested businesses were naturally more efficient than the state.

Elsewhere, private firms were subsidised through workers' tax credits, which effectively enabled employers to resist pay rises for the poorest in society. The drive to the small state continued, in particular with reference to financial goods and services. People amassed considerable amounts of unsecured personal debt, for example on credit cards. They then serviced these by taking out new debts from different providers who themselves offered low or zero costs on balance transfers. In the financial services sector, new ways of classifying debt saw debts categorised as assets. But when, in 2007, it became clear that much of this debt was not an asset but junk, which people could not repay, panicked markets withdrew lines of credit in an attempt to not be caught holding large amounts of bad debt. The shock to the global finance sector was enormous, precipitating the credit crunch of 2007–2008 and the recession that followed it, as we will see in Chapter Eleven. Neoliberal ideas had come to dominate the ideas that rule us, but without the attempts of the social democratic state to ameliorate capitalism's inherent instability – which had been identified as long ago as Marx's time – they had become destructive to the economic system they supported and the people who lived under them. The shift in the gambling industry away from the responsibility of the state to protect people from problem gambling, to a belief in the individual's right to spend their money how they wanted, was a prime example of how free market fundamentalism came to replace social democracy. By the end of the New Labour era, Thatcher's belief that there was 'no such thing as society' wasn't far off the mark. It was little wonder that when asked what her greatest achievement had been, Thatcher had replied 'New Labour'. The feeling was mutual; reflecting back on Thatcher's legacy, Blair commented, 'Many of the things she said, even though they pained people like me on the left... had a certain creditability.'[13]

Notes

1 The ideas were worked out in Anthony Giddens, *Beyond Left and Right* (Cambridge, Polity, 1994) and crystallised at the time of New Labour coming to power in Anthony Giddens, *The Third Way: The Renewal of Social Democracy* (Cambridge, Polity, 1998).
2 A useful way of seeing the scale of the problem is via the maps produced by the *Guardian* as part of an investigation into raw sewage discharges, Niels de Hoog, "'Unacceptable': How Raw Sewage Has Affected Rivers in England and Wales – in Maps", *The Guardian*, 12 September 2023, https://www.theguardian.com/environment/ng-interactive/2023/sep/12/unacceptable-how-raw-sewage-has-affected-rivers-in-england-and-wales-in-maps (accessed 28 February 2024).
3 Tony Blair, "We Won't Look Back to the 1970s", *The Times*, 31 March 1997.
4 The quotation is sometimes selectively quoted, as Mandelson confirmed in a letter to the *Guardian* on 12 June 2008. The quotation is from a speech Mandelson gave to computer executives in California in 1998.
5 "A Safe Bet for Success – Modernising Britain's Gambling Laws", Department for Culture, Media and Sport (London, HMSO, 26 March 2002).
6 "The Government's Proposals for Gambling: Nothing to Lose", Department for Culture, Media and Sport (London, HMSO, 17 July 2002).
7 Ibid.
8 John Woodhouse, "Fixed Odds Betting Terminals", 2019, Briefing Paper, House of Commons Library.
9 Rob Davies, "Number of Problem Gamblers in the UK Rises to More than 400,000", *The Guardian*, 24 August 2017.
10 Randeep Ramesh, "High-Stakes Gambling Machines 'Suck Money from Poorest Communities'", *The Guardian*, 4 January 2013.
11 Alayna Murray, et al. "Autism, Problematic Internet Use and Gaming Disorder: A Systematic Review", *Review Journal of Autism and Developmental Disorders* 9, no. 1, 2021: 120–140.
12 The wording of the petition is still available at https://www.petitiononline.uk/back_your_bookies (accessed 28 February 2024).
13 "Tony Blair: 'My Job was to Build on Some Thatcher Policies'", *BBC News*, 8 April 2013, https://www.bbc.co.uk/news/av/uk-politics-22073434 (accessed 27 March 2024).

References

"A Safe Bet for Success – Modernising Britain's Gambling Laws", Department for Culture, Media and Sport (London, HMSO, 26 March 2002).
"The Government's Proposals for Gambling: Nothing to Lose", Department for Culture, Media and Sport (London, HMSO, 17 July 2002).
"Tony Blair: 'My Job was to Build on Some Thatcher Policies'", *BBC News*, 8 April 2013, https://www.bbc.co.uk/news/av/uk-politics-22073434 (accessed 27 March 2024).

Blair, T. "We Won't Look Back to the 1970s", *The Times*, 31 March 1997.

Davies, R. "Number of Problem Gamblers in the UK Rises to More than 400,000", *The Guardian*, 24 August 2017.

de Hoog, N. "'Unacceptable': How Raw Sewage Has Affected Rivers in England and Wales – in Maps", *The Guardian*, 12 September 2023, https://www.thegua rdian.com/environment/ng-interactive/2023/sep/12/unacceptable-how-raw-sewage -has-affected-rivers-in-england-and-wales-in-maps (accessed 28 February 2024).

Giddens, A. *Beyond Left and Right* (Cambridge, Polity, 1994).

Giddens, A. *The Third Way: The Renewal of Social Democracy* (Cambridge, Polity, 1998).

Murray, A, et al. "Autism, Problematic Internet Use and Gaming Disorder: A Systematic Review", *Review Journal of Autism and Developmental Disorders* 9, no. 1, 2021: 120–140.

Ramesh, R. "High-Stakes Gambling Machines 'Suck Money from Poorest Communities'", *The Guardian*, 4 January 2013.

Woodhouse, J. "Fixed Odds Betting Terminals", 2019, Briefing Paper, House of Commons Library.

11

THE KEYNESIAN FOXHOLE

The final three years of the New Labour government were dominated by the financial crisis of 2007–2008. As we will see here, the crisis was centred on the financial sector of the United States, but so deep was the crisis there that the global economy began to collapse. Banks in the US and Britain faltered and had to be propped up whilst others failed completely. In Iceland, all three of the country's banks collapsed and had to be nationalised. Likewise in the UK, most of the major banks were part-nationalised whilst the Northern Rock bank had to be fully nationalised due to being insolvent. We saw the effects of the crisis on Greece (with similar stories in Italy, Spain, Portugal, and Ireland) in Chapter Eight. At first, governments responded to the crisis by hoping that the markets would correct themselves, but the contagion spread throughout the global economy. When the fourth-largest investment bank in the US, Lehman Brothers, filed for bankruptcy, it seemed that people were living in times reminiscent of the Wall Street Crash. Governments resolved to step in to correct these market failures. Bailouts and nationalisations had the look of a return to Keynesianism. However, as we will see, what eventually occurred was not support for demand in the form of ensuring the needs of workers were met through social democratic means, but rather ensuring that banks remained afloat using money from government-issued debt which, subsequently, austerity economics attempted to make ordinary people pay back.[1]

DOI: 10.4324/9781003161950-11

Causes of the Crisis

The failure of so many banks in the 1930s, alongside the loss of depositors' money, led to governments around the world regulating the banking sector in such a way as to lessen risks to ordinary people. In the US, this took the form of the Glass–Steagall Act of 1933. The Act effectively separated investment banks from commercial banks (those banks that everyday depositors might use to hold their savings or wages). The idea was to prevent the situation which occurred after the Wall Street Crash where banks' losses on investments sent them under, and with them the deposits of savers. The Act also created the Federal Deposit Insurance Corporation which used money sourced collectively from banks to insure people's deposits. But during the 1980s and 1990s, the regulation of the US investment and commercial banking systems was, in the spirit of neoliberal deregulation, slowly chipped away at. In 1999, the Glass–Steagall Act was effectively repealed, allowing investment banks to make investments in mortgage lenders, and allowing commercial banks to engage in the kinds of speculation that had previously been restricted to the investment banks.

At the same time, there was also a rapid increase in the amount of debt being issued in the US economy. Much like in the UK, banks had been handing out easy credit to borrowers, in the years up to 2007–2008. This was because deregulation had created dangerous competition amongst lenders. People would max out a credit card, and then look around for a deal – such as transferring the debt to another provider on a one-year, interest-free balance transfer offer. In the housing market, where prices were growing rapidly, it became possible for people to remortgage their houses at levels above the value of the house and then use the money raised to undertake renovations (or, for that matter, just to fund a blowout). Part of the cause of the growth in house prices was the growth of the buy-to-let market for mortgages. Mortgage lenders also reduced their insistence on relatively high deposit levels for access to credit, using smaller – or no – deposit mortgages to attract borrowers. In some cases, lenders would offer mortgages where people simply paid the interest on the mortgage, making no headway into the actual sum of money borrowed to buy the property in the first place.[2]

Riskier deals on mortgages led to what became known as the sub-prime mortgage crisis. In the years before 2007, mortgages were issued during a boom in house prices that, from 2007, turned into a decline.

People on variable-term mortgages had been tempted into home ownership by initial deals on mortgages that included a lower, or no,
deposit. They were also offered initial lower interest rates, which were
then followed by the interest rate increasing to the market rate. For
those who could only just meet the repayment rates of the initial deal,
this meant that they could either find the money elsewhere or sell the
house. But the problem was that as house prices fell, selling up would
not solve people's problem as they found themselves in negative equity.
Instead of being able to remortgage to another provider for a similarly
cheap deal, as many had planned, homeowners found themselves in
houses not worth the mortgage they were paying and unable to sell to
escape the steep repayment rates. Unsurprisingly, many defaulted. As
houses that had been defaulted on went back on the market, prices went
down further, bringing others into negative equity.

The sub-prime mortgage selling scandal was a tragedy for those who
were convinced to take on mortgages they were very unlikely to be able
to service, and lost considerable amounts of money along the way. In
the US it was also a tragedy that fell more heavily on black borrowers,
who were far more likely than white borrowers to have fallen victim to
predatory mortgage lending at clearly unsustainable rates of interest.
But personal tragedy turned to global economic crisis. This was because
deregulation had allowed banks to trade mortgages as assets. Mortgages
were bundled together with other mortgages and sold off as bonds. The
idea was that the bonds would include low-risk debt alongside higher-
risk debt. Investors bought those parts of the bond they were comfor-
table taking a risk on. Relatively low-risk parts of the bond returned
lower rates than their riskier counterparts. Also, the bond contained
mortgages from across the US, the idea being that, whilst someone
might default on a mortgage in one part of the country, there was no
reason to believe that would be accompanied by defaults elsewhere.
After all, America is a big place and it wasn't expected that the housing
market could slump across the board.

Once packaged up, mortgage bonds were then traded between the
various investment banks. Some of these bonds may have changed
hands as many as six or seven times. Of course, we know now that
these bonds contained much more of the sub-prime mortgages then
investors knew at the time. As the housing market started to decline,
and defaults on mortgages increased, the safety of these bonds was
downgraded by the major credit rating agencies. On the eve of the

crisis, investors were uncertain as to just how much junk debt they were sitting on top of. Worse still, they weren't sure how much junk debt other banks were sitting on either. Unsurprisingly, banks that either were sitting on unknown amounts of debt, or else didn't know which other banks were still good bets, stopped lending money whilst they worked out what kind of situation they were in. But, as we saw above, many people were using cheap credit in order to service their debts. Once cheap credit dried up, defaults on unsecured debts, such as credit cards, were inevitable. That was pretty dire for ordinary people. But in the finance sector, something similar was also going on. Investors had been buying up housing market bonds using short-term credit. When short-term lending dried up or became much more expensive, this short-term debt could only be serviced by selling off mortgage portfolios. This took time, which was a problem if large amounts of money were needed fast to repay debts that were due, and, of course, worsened the crisis as more houses entered the market.

One of the first signs that there was a problem in the UK in 2007 was when the Northern Rock bank found itself in dire trouble.[3] Northern Rock was a bank that was heavily invested in the UK mortgage market, and the majority of the money which it used to fund this did not come from deposits from savers, but from borrowing. It was not that technically speaking the bank was insolvent. Its assets did cover its liabilities. However, when interbank lending started to dry up, Northern Rock found itself unable to raise the money it needed to pay off debts that were becoming payable because most of its money was invested in mortgages. Its share price tumbled as shareholders worried the bank might have to default on debts. To try to get around this problem, initially, Northern Rock borrowed around £3 billion from the Bank of England to pay its debts whilst trying to sell off its assets so that it held enough cash to meet its obligations. Of course, this was all public knowledge. People who had money in Northern Rock worried that the bank might not be able to produce the money held in their accounts. Queues formed outside of the bank's branches as people tried to withdraw their savings. But this just made the problem worse; once there was a run on the bank, it really couldn't raise enough money quickly enough to pay depositors. The government attempted to stem the panic by increasing its guarantee on funds held by banks from £35,000 to £85,000, though to some extent this seemed something of an admission of a serious problem, making people's enthusiasm to get their money out even greater. To counter this, the Treasury guaranteed all deposits in the bank. Queues subsided. By the time the panic ended, the Bank of England had loaned Northern Rock around £30 billion and guaranteed around £25 billion of the bank's deposits. As the mortgage portfolio of around £50 billion likely contained significant amounts of junk debt, the government took that on too which nationalised Northern Rock in all but name.

Northern Rock's fall did not affect the US market, but it should have served as a warning because this issue was just as likely to happen to US banks. Problems in the US banking sector emerged in 2007 when two large hedge funds run by the Bear Stearns investment bank went bust. These then had to be bailed out by operations in the rest of the bank. It was a first sign that the mortgage bonds which people had been trading were less secure than previously thought. The credit rating agencies downgraded Bear Stearns, and by March 2008, it had run out of cash and was sitting on an investment portfolio that was ruined by the decline of the housing market. Because of the size of the losses, the US government felt it had no option but to rescue the bank by taking its bad debt off it. What was left was sold to another bank, JP Morgan Chase. Naturally, investors began to wonder who would fail next. Lehman Brothers investment bank had invested heavily in mortgage securities. Like they had with Bear Stearns, investors wondered if this meant the bank could meet its liabilities and started to withdraw funds, leading, again, to the need to sell off mortgage securities in a declining market. By September 2008, it had nearly run out of cash, and its shares had plummeted to rock bottom. On 15 September, Lehman Brothers declared bankruptcy.

Unlike Northern Rock or Bear Stearns, Lehman Brothers was not nationalised. This proved to be an error on the part of the US government. Lehman Brothers was, after all, the fourth-largest bank in America. If it was not considered to be too big to fail, then that would apply to most other banks. A credit crunch set in as banks stopped lending and began investing in government debt (known as Treasury Bonds in the US and Gilts in the UK). It wasn't so much that there was 'no more money', just that no one was willing to lend what they had. In a system that had come to depend on credit to keep running, this was disastrous. Governments in the US and Britain, along with the European Central Bank, pumped money into their economies to ease the effect of the credit crunch. By the time the dust settled, the US insurer American

International Group, one of the largest companies in the world, which had insured significant amounts of the mortgage debt against default, was bailed out by the US government to the tune of $180 billion. Iceland's banking sector collapsed, the three major national Irish banks required bailouts, and all UK banks with the exception of Barclays and HSBC required bailouts. Ireland, Hungary, and Greece required IMF bailouts as a result of trying to save their banking sectors (or, ironically, in the case of Greece, as we saw in Chapter Eight, trying to save the banking sectors of France and Germany).

It is hard to fully capture the outcome of the financial crisis of 2007–2008. As we will see in Chapter Twelve, the crisis allowed a narrative to emerge that favoured a small state whose focus was on business rather than supporting society more broadly. As we saw in Chapter Eight, in the case of Greece the bailouts cost the people there some of their democratic rights. The results of this, we will see, were disastrous and failed to restore the economy to health. In terms of hard cash, the political economist Mark Blyth points out that the cost to the US was somewhere around $9 trillion. And in the UK, the Treasury had to spend around 12.5% of the UK's GDP on the bank rescues. Blyth is absolutely right to insist that these sums were the cost of the crisis, not the cause of it.[4]

The Great Recession

As the dust settled on the world economy, it was inevitable that a recession would follow. Governments were in a considerably more interventionist mood than in the previous years of neoliberalism. Robert Lucas, an economist whose ideas reinforced neoliberalism, declared, 'I guess everyone is a Keynesian in a foxhole.' He went on: 'but I don't think we are there yet.'[5] Lucas' argument was that, whilst the post-crash recession was bad, it wasn't so bad that government needed to return to interventions in the market. Who knows if he was right, but it seems far-fetched that governments could have let the global finance and banking system collapse and find a new equilibrium without the whole edifice of capitalism collapsing too. It is little surprise that the British Prime Minister, Gordon Brown, whose doctoral thesis had been on interwar politics, advocated intervention to save the economy.[6]

To try to rescue the global economy from the after-effects of the crash, the G20 countries agreed to work together to stimulate demand.

This was vital. In Britain, real wages declined by 6% between 2008 and 2014, the worst decline since the 1860s when the American Civil War had starved Lancashire's cotton mills of raw cotton. There was little incentive to invest in labour-saving technology, least of all because of higher unemployment. Worse still, those in work were increasingly facing precarious conditions, characterised most by zero hours contracts. The sight of branches of Domino's Pizza paying people to walk around with an A-board to advertise their pizzas rather than investing in social media advertising tells you all you need to know about how bad wages were. To stimulate global demand, the G20 pledged $1.1 trillion of global stimulus.[7]

Technically speaking, a recession occurs when two or more consecutive quarters of GDP growth are negative. In this sense, countries began to come out of the recession in mid-2009. But the technical description doesn't really do the long-lasting effects justice. Certainly, Britain's economy did not recover the growth knocked off by the crash, and this was made worse first by austerity, then by Brexit, and then by Covid. But the stimulus that had been used under New Labour was ended by the incoming coalition government in 2010. Making the problem worse by cutting government spending – a classic paradox of thrift – the coalition government's economic policy, one of so-called austerity, snatched defeat from the jaws of victory and ushered in what was to be, economically, a dismal decade.

Conclusion

As the crisis of 2007–2008 unfolded, Gordon Brown remembered the ideas of John Maynard Keynes well. Brown argued that the G20 group, representing the 20 most advanced global economies, needed to pump money into the global economy to prevent a crisis of demand caused by people and businesses not spending, and to prevent the losses of the finance and banking sectors dragging down all those who depended upon their successful operation. This stimulus included, in large measure, enormous cash injections to support struggling banks and investment companies. Banks were bailed out, whilst Northern Rock was nationalised to prevent its collapse. The lesson that should have been drawn from the whole debacle was not that the state is inefficient and should leave the market alone, but that, rather, deregulation of banking and finance had elevated personal greed to an unchecked position. Rather than acting in the interests of society, or even the economy, as a whole, clever financial instruments had allowed individuals in the banking and finance sector to make large sums of money. When the whole thing collapsed, it was the state that had to step in and stabilise things, and the people who paid the tab. But not only did people pay the tab for the banks, there was no debt forgiveness for those who lost their houses or who were sitting on large chunks of credit card debt. By contrast, irresponsible and predatory lending by banks was forgiven on the grounds that they were too big to fail. Furthermore, as we will see in the next chapter, in 2010 the banks' profligacy was to be paid for by a nation's austerity.

Notes

1 For a good overview of the crisis, see Linda Yueh, *The Great Crashes* (London, Viking, 2023). For a longer treatment, see Adam Tooze, *Crashed: How a Decade of Financial Crises Changed the World* (London, Allen Lane, 2018).
2 See Tooze, *Crashed*, chapter 5 for the sub-prime scandal as well as William Quinn and John D. Turner, *Boom and Bust: A Global History of Financial Bubbles* (Cambridge, Cambridge University Press, 2020), chapter 11.
3 For bank bailouts see Tooze, *Crashed*, chapter 6.
4 In Mark Blyth, *Austerity: The History of a Dangerous Idea* (Oxford, Oxford University Press, 2018), Blyth emphatically and quite properly makes the case that the government debt which politicians talked about extensively at the time was a reaction to the banking crisis – not its cause.
5 Justin Fox, "The Comeback Keynes", *Time*, 27 January 2009.
6 Gordon Brown, "Labour Party and Political Change in Scotland, 1918–1929: The Politics of Five Elections" (PhD thesis, University of Edinburgh, 1982).
7 For the stimulus see Tooze, *Crashed*, chapters 11 and 12.

References

Blyth, M. *Austerity: The History of a Dangerous Idea* (Oxford, Oxford University Press, 2018).
Brown, G. "*Labour Party and Political Change in Scotland, 1918–1929: The Politics of Five Elections*" (PhD thesis, University of Edinburgh, 1982).
Fox, J. "The Comeback Keynes", *Time*, 27 January 2009.
Quinn, W. and Turner, J. D. *Boom and Bust: A Global History of Financial Bubbles* (Cambridge, Cambridge University Press, 2020).
Tooze, A. *Crashed: How a Decade of Financial Crises Changed the World* (London, Allen Lane, 2018).
Yueh, L. *The Great Crashes: Lessons from Global Meltdowns and How to Prevent Them* (London, Penguin, 2023).

12

AUSTERITY AND THE NATION'S CREDIT CARD

The object of austerity economics, introduced by the UK Conservative-led government in 2010, was, contrary to Keynes, to restore the economy to growth through cutting government expenditure. The idea was simple; the government argued that the crisis of 2007–2008 had come about because easy access to personal debt that turned bad had destabilised the financial sector. Just as households had to cut their cloth to the new post-credit crunch world, so too must government. The moral justification for this was that it was unfair to run up long-term government debt that future generations would need to repay. The economic justification was that lower expenditure would mean tax cuts, putting money in the pockets of businesses so that they could invest in expanding their operations and in new, more productive, technologies. And a small number of economists argued that countries with large ratios of debt to GDP faced stalled growth in the future, justifying sustained attempts to reduce the UK national debt. To many, this was common sense. After all, people re-elected the Conservatives in 2015, 2017, and 2019.[1] Yet, the results were disastrous. In this chapter we see the ideas borrowed from mainstream economics which underpinned the policy of austerity. We also examine austerity's unintended results: the UK entered over a decade of declining real wages, experienced a slump in productivity, and witnessed an enormous growth in the national debt.

DOI: 10.4324/9781003161950-12

'There is no More Money'

We saw in Chapter Eleven that the 2007–2008 financial crisis was a systemic one originating in the banking sector. Banks were holding unknown amounts of junk debt. When they realised this, they stopped lending and started calling in debts. Not only did this restrict borrowing for businesses, but also for individuals. For individuals sitting on a lot of personal debt, access to more funds was increasingly essential in the years running up to the crisis. People had been dealing with lots of credit card debt by moving providers, using zero-interest balance transfers. Once these dried up, people were no longer able to pay their debts. In the run-up to the 2010 election, the Conservatives reimagined the causes of the 2007–2008 financial crisis. Turning outcomes into causes, they argued that it was people's excessive use of personal debt, combined with government overspending, which had caused the crisis. But, of course, government debt was actually a result of the necessary government spending required *after* the crisis had occurred, and the main crisis was actually in the sub-prime mortgage market.[2] This reimagining led the Conservatives to the conclusion that the problem was too much debt, and that the solution was people and government spending less and paying off debt.

As the economist Simon Wren-Lewis has argued, the run-up to the 2010 election saw the tide turn against the spending measures Gordon Brown's government had taken at home and had advocated for overseas.[3] Bodies such as the IMF, European Central Bank, and World Bank began to argue for balanced budgets and a reduction in national debt. To not do so might provoke 'nervous' financial markets to withdraw the finance that was so essential in preventing a return to the credit crunch of the crisis years which, with official recessions having ended in 2009, appeared to be behind us. The right-wing press, keen to see its readership provided with tax cuts, weighed in, repeating the Conservative mantra that it was excessive government spending that had provoked the crisis in the first place. By doing so, they justified another push at the small-state agenda that had slowed (though certainly not stopped) in the New Labour years. The *Daily Telegraph* even launched an attack on Wren-Lewis for pointing out the obvious truth that government debt in the run-up to 2007 had not provoked the crisis and that raising funds to overcome the recession the crisis had caused made good financial sense.

Upon Labour's defeat in the 2010 election, Liam Byrne wrote a short note to his successor which read, 'There is no more money, I'm afraid.' He was making a joke. It is a tradition stretching back to the 1960s that the outgoing First Secretary to the Treasury leaves a self-deprecating but amusing note for their successor. But the joke backfired, and Byrne has regretted it ever since.[4] In the years after 2010, the right-wing press kept up the idea that Labour's economic policies had caused the crash and subsequent recession. As austerity grew more entrenched as an economic idea, the Labour Party, rather than challenging this, merely accepted it and fought the 2015 election on the premise that further austerity was necessary. In that election, David Cameron, the then Prime Minister, paraded Byrne's note up and down the country. His message was clear: Labour had, by 2010, near-bankrupted the country and only further austerity would be able to put it back on a good financial standing.

Repeated austerity was the message throughout the years of the coalition government. Time and again in the government's early years, Chancellor George Osborne argued that unless the cuts to government spending begun in 2010 were continued, and the national debt reduced, Britain would soon turn into an economy similar to that of Greece (we saw in Chapter Eight that Greece was bankrupt in 2010 and had to be bailed out in 2010, 2012, and 2015). Signalling this right from the start, in 2010, the government argued that previous spending plans were out of control and had to be reined in. The Department for Work and Pensions issued a statement declaring, 'The welfare bill has become unsustainably expensive... 1.4 million [people] have been receiving out-of-work benefits for nine out of the last ten years... 1.9 million children [are] living in homes where no-one has a job.'[5] Austerity's message was a return to the idea that it was the feckless poor who were bringing the country down, taking money from more 'honest' folk. From 2007–2008 the country had blamed the bankers for the mess people found themselves in. By 2010, the Conservatives decided that it was time to push back. This was around the time that Boris Johnson made his 'knighthoods for zillionaires' statement, which we saw in Chapter Two.

Now, let us have a look at the theory behind austerity.

Austerity Economics

So far in this book, we have explored the idea that in a deep recession the best thing that the state can do is inject money into the economy to stimulate demand. This looked especially necessary in the aftermath of the 2007–2008 crisis given that credit was hard to come by, and, as we saw in Chapter Eleven, this was the policy which the New Labour government under Gordon Brown followed. Yet, a small group of economists produced an idea that challenged this. For example, Alberto Alesina and Silvia Ardagna argued that it would be possible to grow the economy by reducing government spending and taxation.[6] 'Fiscal consolidations' (as Alesina and Ardagna technically described austerity) could, theoretically, lead to a growth of output (GDP) in the economy. By reducing spending and therefore the need for higher tax revenues, the government would free up businesses to invest in new products and services which would, through innovation, grow the economy. They called this 'expansionary contraction' because the idea was that less spending would grow the economy. Since national debt is usually measured as the amount of government debt relative to GDP, whilst the actual headline figure of the debt itself might not shrink, as a percentage of GDP the national debt would decrease as GDP grew.

In addition to Alesina and Ardagna's argument on expansionary contraction, two other economists, Carmen Reinhart and Kenneth Rogoff, produced a paper relating to government debt called 'Growth in a Time of Debt'.[7] Reinhart and Rogoff argued that when a country's debt to GDP ratio reached 90%, further GDP growth would be halved compared to if the ratio was below 60%. In 2010, the UK's debt to GDP ratio was at around 75%, which Reinhart and Rogoff argued would have a negative influence on growth, and by 2015 it was nearing the 90% ratio. So, in addition to cutting taxes to stimulate growth, the coalition government and its successor set about trying to raise a surplus to pay down the national debt.

The concept of austerity was too good to be true. For government it held out the promise of being able to reduce public and business taxes, grow the economy, and decrease the national debt. New Labour, under Brown, had tried a limited attempt at tax relief to encourage businesses in 2008 by reducing the corporate tax rate from 30% to 28%. The coalition government went much further. By 2015, the rate was as low as 20%, falling, in 2017, under Theresa May's government, to 19%.

In terms of cutting government expenditure, public sector employment was cut. The number of public sector employees jumped in 2008 to 5.25 million (because of bank nationalisations) but by 2017 was down at around 4.4 million, the lowest number of public sector employees in the economy since 2000, and it fell further still in 2018. At the same time, there was a 1% cap on wage increases in the public sector; a reduction in government services, particularly ones aimed at prevention of social problems; and even those areas of government that the Conservatives had traditionally supported such as policing were cut, with just over 120,000 officers in 2010 being reduced to just over 100,000 by 2018.

The Trade Union Act 2016

Alesina and Ardagna had been arguing for austerity as long ago as the late 1990s and early 2000s. Both were academic economists at Harvard Business School, until, in 2007, Ardagna went to work for the Bank of America. By 2010, when Alesina and Ardagna published an article that made them leading proponents of austerity, and provided the Conservative Party with the academic justification they needed for abandoning Labour's fiscal policies and doubling down on the neo-liberal-style small state, Ardagna had moved to the investment banking company Goldman Sachs (via the Bank of America). Little wonder they were keen to advocate for tax cuts for private business and the further shrinking of the state.

Alongside the arguments for 'expansionary contraction', Alesina and Ardagna also argued that trade unions needed to play a specific role in the economy if austerity were to work. Their argument was that for austerity to work, trade unions would need to cooperate with government to achieve its economic policy. In an economic downturn, organised labour would normally be expected to advocate for government investment to retain and create jobs, and in the case of rising inflation, call for wage increases to match the higher cost of living. Under austerity, trade unions would have to accept that to boost the ability of businesses to invest, workers would have to take lower wages (given that the point was that the state would not provide that investment). The argument ran that though this would result in a short-term squeeze for workers, in the medium term the economy would grow to the benefit of all. Two ways in which the government can act to shrink wages in the economy are, first, cut jobs in the public sector (increasing unemployment, therefore making competition for jobs harder so that employers can pay less) and, second, hold down, as far as possible, public sector wages. Alesina and Ardagna proposed that either trade unions should be persuaded that this was a good plan that would work, or else government should use legal means to restrict the rights ('power', as the right-wing press would put it) of trade unions.

Interestingly, Alesina also considered the political consequences of public sector wage cuts and job losses. He argued that these would not necessarily be a problem for governments at the ballot box but might still meet concerted resistance 'because such policies go against the interests of entrenched bureaucracies'.[8] It might be too kind to suggest that Michael Gove had read some economics, but this outcome that Alesina identified does chime with Gove's references to 'the blob' during the 2013 teachers' strikes. Gove, then education secretary, was echoing his US counterpart from the early 1980s, William Bennett, who used the derogatory term 'blob' to describe civil servants, educationalists, and researchers who opposed reforms of terms and conditions and changes to teaching practice.[9] (Bennett himself was, in turn, channelling the 1950s film *The Blob*, but this is not necessarily relevant given that no one thinks alien monsters are running the government, apart from David Ike, of course.) Gove attempted to weaponise the 'blob' to overcome objections to his plans for education. By vilifying education professionals, Gove was trying to open up a space where his plans for a learn-by-rote curriculum, extended school days, staffing cuts, and real wages decreases would be welcomed. It played well to bodies such as the TaxPayers' Alliance and the Institute for Economic Affairs. Some years later, in the fallout from Brexit where most economists predicted that the outcome of Britain's leaving the EU would be an economic downturn, Gove went further and declared, 'I think the people of this country have all had enough of experts.'[10] What Alesina, and Gove for that matter, were focussing on attacking here wasn't so much the state itself (though there are plenty of libertarians who would do just that) but rather vestiges of social democracy that have yet to be purged from it.

Alesina may well have been right in arguing that governments that sold themselves as being staunch on fiscal contraction do not suffer too greatly at the ballot box if they show themselves as being serious about economic reforms to reduce deficits. In 2015, the Conservative Party was able to shed its coalition with the Liberal Democrats after a general election that gave them a majority in parliament (whilst at the same time the Liberal Democrats were punished by their voters, being, nearly, wiped out as a parliamentary party). Soon after, the Conservative government introduced legislation to restrict the ability of trade unions to call industrial action. In 2016, the Trade Union Act passed into law. It required that industrial action could only be called if 50% of trade union members participated in the ballot for industrial action. For some sectors this was also made harder by a requirement that the vote for strike action be voted for by 40% of all eligible voters in the ballot (in addition to making the 50% turnout threshold). It also introduced a two-week notice period before trade unions could begin industrial action and limited the length of time during which action could be taken to within six months of the original ballot (or, laughably, nine months if the employer agreed to it).

The effect of the 2016 Trade Union Act has been to change the way in which people engage in strike ballots. For example, unions that tend to get a high turnout in ballots tend to have a large percentage in favour of strike action. It has become more effective for those who do not want to go on strike not to vote, rather than to vote no. It's hard to say if the Act has reduced the amount of industrial action taken, which we can measure to some extent by looking at the number of working days lost to strike action. Figures in the year immediately after 2016 were low but comparable to the previous years. Nevertheless, since June 2022 there has been a considerable increase in working days lost to strike action. And in the face of the cost-of-living crisis kicked off by the Russian war in Ukraine, industrial action by public sector workers has certainly seen government attempt to restrict further organised labour.[11] The 2023 Strikes (Minimal Services) Act set out to restrict who, in key services, could take industrial action. Those designated by the Business Secretary as being required to attend work to provide minimal levels of cover during industrial action cannot refuse to do so and retain legal protections. Unions that fail to provide such minimal levels of service could be sued for losses. Whilst the Act covered health care, nuclear commissioning, and fire and rescue, the reality was that these industries already operated minimal essential cover during industrial action. After all, it is hardly in the interests of those in the nuclear industry to secure a pay rise by neglecting, say, Sellafield and blowing up half of Lancashire. But the Act does also cover education and transport, and the teachers' strikes, and rail strikes, of 2022 and 2023 were the primary targets of this legislation. It remains to be seen if the Act will be applied to university workers who have taken record-breaking amounts of industrial action since 2016. Or indeed to train drivers who were threatened with enforcement in early 2024 only to have employers back down when their union threatened to escalate industrial action in response – much to the Prime Minister Rishi Sunak's disappointment.[12]

Results

Austerity economics was, indeed, too good to be true. The cap on public sector pay increases served to stifle demand due to inflation hammering down real wages. The reduction in government spending, at just the moment that the UK economy was entering recession, dampened demand and undermined businesses. It took from 2010 to 2019 for real wages to return to the levels they had been at before the financial crisis. Everyone suffered from a reduction in public services, though naturally those who relied on state provision of transport, health care, and social security suffered more greatly. If cutting taxes was intended to create a trickle-down of wealth, it certainly did not find its way to the homeless. The number of rough sleepers in the UK grew from 1768 per night in 2010 to a peak of 4751 in 2017, after which it fell slightly, though at 2688 in 2020 it was still much higher than in 2010.[13] Lockdown measures to combat Covid helped to bring some people indoors (though numbers had not gone down below pre-financial crisis levels). Likewise, children have not seen benefits from austerity, with the child poverty rate higher in 2020–2021 than at the height of the financial crisis.

Austerity did not even achieve good outcomes on its own terms. The national debt ballooned from 60% of GDP in 2010 to around 80% of GDP pre-Covid. At the start of the crisis, the debt, excluding the public sector banks, stood at less than £1 trillion. By 2023 it had more than doubled to £2.5 trillion, 96% of GDP.[14] Nor did it reduce household debt. In fact, it reduced opportunities for full-time work. Combined with declining welfare provision and real wages, personal debt increased. In household terms, this meant that whereas household debt in 2010 stood on average at £8287 per household, by 2019 it was at £12,766 per household.[15] And whilst the unemployment rate fell from a peak in 2010, back to pre-crisis levels by 2019, what remained stubbornly high was the underemployment rate – the number of those looking for more work. The lack of work meant that not only did household debt increase but also household savings declined, a crucial buffer against the reduction of social security, as people struggled to keep up with bills. By 2016, saving levels were lower than they had been at any time since 2000.[16]

But even if the debt reduction goals of austerity had not been achieved, had it nevertheless restored the UK economy? How do you define an economic recovery? As the economist Simon Wren-Lewis puts it so well, you have two choices of definition. Imagine a running race. A runner falls. Have they recovered when they stand up and begin running again, or have they recovered when they have caught up with the other runners? Wren-Lewis argues that it is when the runner has caught up with the others.[17] And on these terms, austerity has been a chronic failure. GDP growth per head not only has nearly flatlined but is now far behind where it should be had growth continued at the same rate as during 1955–2007. Similarly, productivity in the UK flatlined between 2010 and 2016, then began to increase between 2017 and 2020, before flatlining again. It remains well below where it should have been had it continued to grow as it had from 1970 to the outbreak of the financial crisis.[18]

Why Did Austerity Fail?

Despite the support for austerity from a few economists, the reality was that most could see that this policy would fail. The rejection of Keynesian solutions for combatting peaks and troughs in the economy meant that, particularly under New Labour, government focussed on monetary policy to keep the economy in a sustainable position of growth, with inflation lying at around 2%. When inflation rose because the economy was doing too well (overheating), interest rates rose. Likewise, in a downturn, rates fell to stimulate growth. Before the financial crisis this worked reasonably well and prompted Gordon Brown, when Chancellor under Tony Blair, to declare that there would be no return to the 'boom and bust' era of the previous Conservative administrations. The financial crisis ended that period of relative stability, however.

On the eve of the crisis, the Bank of England base rate was 5.5%. To combat the economic downturn, the rate was lowered to 2% in 2008, then to 0.5% until 2016 when it was reduced further to 0.25%. Low figures such as those are at what is called the zero lower bound – the point below which it is not possible to go (see Chapter Four). Of course, the zero lower bound is not a fixed thing. Japan went into negative interest rates to combat its recession, but this did not work and for the Conservatives, who rely on votes from older people with savings, this would have been electorally damaging. So, for practical reasons we can say that in the years of austerity interest rates were at the zero lower bound. The question then becomes, 'What else could be done?' And if you have ruled out using fiscal policy – government spending – as austerity had, then the answer is 'not much'. At that point, we are back to waiting in the long run for the market to correct itself (for Keynes' attitude on the long run see Chapter Five).

Part of the problem was the very framing that the coalition government put on its austerity policies. In the run-up to the 2010 election, David Cameron spoke extensively of the 'nation's credit card', which he argued had been maxed out. This metaphorical linking of government and household debt had negative consequences for the economy. Cameron's image of a reckless and profligate nation spending too much provoked householders into paying off debt rather than spending. The decrease in demand threatened to worsen the crisis and the government was forced to backtrack on the idea. But more important than those immediate unintended consequences is the idea that government finances are like those of a household. In fact, they are not.

Households spend their income. We receive money, say, through wages, and then we spend throughout the week or month until more money comes our way. We might use a credit card to allow us to make a big purchase and spread the cost of that purchase over future months. We might also save some money for future purchases, pensions, or just for a rainy day. Austerity tries to make government finances out to be the same – tax money comes in, the government spends. If it spends too much, it gets into debt and eventually it is the people that will have to pay the debt off. But for government, none of this is really the case. At the start of the government's financial year, it estimates its costs for the following year. It then raises the money to pay for this by issuing debt, in other words inviting people to give the government money in return for bonds which pay a certain percentage per year and eventually return also the price paid. These bonds can be short-term bonds, or have terms of 5, 10, or 20 years. At times, the UK government has even issued bonds that have no expiry date, and which were passed down from one generation to another.[19]

Tax is not spent by the government to fund things like the NHS; government pays for that through borrowing. Tax simply pays the interest on the debt which government uses to pay for its expenditure. It can also be used to pay off the initial value of the bonds too. But in a recession, that is not really what you want to do because people actually want to buy government debt in difficult times. When financial markets are in turmoil – remember that banks went under during the crisis – people with money want safe harbours to invest it in. And, given that the UK government simply cannot go bankrupt because it prints its own currency, the safest option is government debt. So secure is government debt that the returns on it during many years when the base rate was as low as 0.25% were, after accounting for inflation, actually negative. In other words, investors were perfectly happy to pay the government money for the privilege of buying its debt. And this is because the UK prints its own currency. Theresa May was technically correct when she said there is not a magic money tree; instead, there is an ordinary printing press which can produce as much money as is required.

But if in a recession you try to cut down on the amount of debt issued, or worse still start paying back the debt, you need to suck money out of the economy in the form of tax to do so, as well as cutting back expenditure. Naturally, this took demand out of the economy as the government pumped less money into the economy. And with interest rates at the zero lower bound, effectively, government economic policy failed. There was not some miracle investment by businesses because of tax cuts, and with the state not investing in the economy, demand remained too low and productivity boosting investment in technology failed to materialise. Reductions in real wages affected consumption. At first savings covered the gap in people's budgets. Once those were exhausted people once again turned to debt. But with rates being now higher than before the financial crisis, the sustainability of that is questionable.

Had austerity worked, and worked quickly, then the debt to GDP ratio may well have fallen. The problem was that because it did not work, GDP growth remained sluggish. Meanwhile, as we have seen, the government's efforts to lower the amount of debt were ultimately self-defeating. Worse still, the justification for trying to reduce the debt to GDP ratio, by 2013, seemed discredited. In a paper by Herndon, Ash, and Pollin, the data underpinning Reinhart and Rogoff's work were brought into question. They had discovered that there were a series of coding errors in the data used in 'Growth in a Time of Debt', and also argued that significant data which undermined the paper had been excluded or else used selectively.[20] As the economist Paul Krugman put it, Reinhart and Rogoff's work was 'sloppy... This work fell apart on examination, but only after it had served as an excuse for destructive policies in much of Europe.'[21] Indeed. Ideas matter, and they can have dramatic real-world consequences.

Had government invested in the years of austerity, then the UK economy would have been in a much better place to resist the three shocks to the recent economy of Brexit, Covid-19, and the cost-of-living crisis, of which the last had been brewing since 2010 but became a significant problem from the onset of the Russian war in Ukraine. As it is, the legacy of austerity will be ten or more wasted years of poor economic growth and lowered living conditions and dilapidated infrastructure. Rather than a new age under a newly crowned king, the Conservatives have simply served up the reheated grimness of the mid-1990s.

Is Austerity Over?

The austerity years owed much to the ideas that underpinned the neoliberal economic ideas we saw in Chapter Seven. Advocates of austerity began from the idea that it was the state that was the problem. The argument went that politicians are keen to assure themselves of votes and spend too much money in doing so. Much as the crisis in Keynesianism had been in the 1970s, from 2010 this argument was used to justify supply-side solutions to the recession that followed the financial crisis of 2007–2008. In the name of reducing debt, the small state was focussed on. There were privatisations, such as the Royal Mail, as we saw in Chapter Nine. And there were attacks on trade unions, at the same time as tax cuts for the wealthiest in society. And once interest rates were at the zero lower bound, the only answers offered by government were that in the long run the market would correct itself and so in the meantime the best thing to do was to double down on austerity in order to free up the market as much as possible. Meanwhile, there was an expansion of state debt but a further retreat from providing the kinds of services social democracy had dedicated itself towards.

By the time of the 2019 election, austerity had become a political liability. After all, ten years of sluggish growth and a deepening national debt, combined with crumbling public services, were not much to hawk at the ballot box. By contrast, Labour under Jeremy Corbyn was campaigning on the Keynesian-inspired policy of a Green New Deal – government investment in the economy designed to create work and green the economy.[22] In the run-up to the election, the Conservatives inflated their record on the economy and once they were in power, Boris Johnson declared austerity to be over. Government departments were allowed to set above-inflation budgets for the first time since 2010. Tax income was frozen, with no promises to reduce rates as had been the promise under austerity. Months later, the Covid-19 pandemic broke out. At first the government resisted calls for working from home or lockdowns. This was justified by claiming that the main means of transmission was touching infected surfaces or people, rather than through the air. If everyone washed their hands several times a day, taking as long as it takes to sing 'Happy Birthday' twice, all would be OK, Johnson reassured us. It wasn't.

On 23 March 2020, the UK government bowed to the inevitable and introduced lockdown measures that would run, off and on, for around a year. Faced with the collapse of the UK economy, the government introduced its furlough scheme to subsidise wages for those unable to work. It truly did look as though we really were in Robert Lucas's Keynesian foxhole, and that even the Conservative government had had to bend to that. Though this was less than sure. Johnson's support for furlough was lukewarm during the first wave of Covid. Furlough was discontinued in early June 2020 despite many workplaces not being able to operate, but Johnson justified this on the basis that continuing it would prevent the market coming back to equilibrium after its mechanisms were disrupted by the furlough scheme. Subsequently, the government had to roll back on this and on the eve of the second national lockdown the furlough scheme was reintroduced. However, help for small businesses and the millions working in the gig economy was patchy to say the least. Within government, there appeared to be some pulling in different directions. Whereas Johnson stuck closely to his free market view of economic policy, the Treasury seemed more cautious, introducing the 'Eat Out to Help Out' scheme over the summer of 2020 in an attempt to stimulate demand by encouraging people to return to using the hospitality sector (and, in all likelihood, causing the second wave of the pandemic in the UK).

Overall, the response to the Covid schemes, despite mixed views within the cabinet, seems to have been a rejection of austerity and the adoption of Keynesian measures to respond to an economic crisis. But this may be too simple an analysis. For a start, the recovery in the US was much quicker than in the UK because the US government spent more on stimulus (whilst we were eating discounted scotch eggs, US citizens were getting $1000 cheques). And many of the principles of austerity are still with us. Wages have been kept down, particularly in the public sector (but now with inflation as the reason, rather than debt), leading to dramatic real terms cuts in wages. Organised labour is still facing further attacks on its ability to take strike action. Austerity might have been bad economics, but the economic ideas which were used to justify it have successfully furthered the cause of individualism over what is left of social democracy.

Conclusion

Austerity proceeded from a false premise – the idea that the 2007–2008 financial crisis stemmed from governments spending too much. As we saw in the previous chapter, this was not the case. Nevertheless, the idea that 'the nation's credit card' needed to be paid off sent the government down the route of slashing public services and failing to invest in stimulus packages that could have brought the UK out of the Great Recession. In the end, the underpinnings of the idea of austerity came to be unpicked as the work of those economists who advocated austerity came into question. In the next chapter, we look at the world of academic economics to further understand how mainstream economic ideas have become entrenched in our thinking about what is and is not possible in our society.

Notes

1 Though it's worth noting that because of the UK's electoral system, these victories were obtained by persuading only a small minority of those eligible. In 2015, only 11.3 million votes out of an electorate of 46.6 million went to the Conservatives.
2 Mark Blyth, *Austerity: The History of a Dangerous Idea* (Oxford, Oxford University Press, 2018).
3 Simon Wren-Lewis, *The Lies we were Told: Politics, Economics, Austerity and Brexit* (Bristol, Bristol University Press, 2018), 20–23.
4 Liam Byrne, "'I'm Afraid There is no Money'. The Letter I Will Regret For Ever", *The Guardian*, 9 May 2015.
5 "Universal Credit: Welfare that Works", Department for Work and Pensions (Cm 7957, 2010).
6 Alberto Alesina and Silvia Ardagna, "Tales of Fiscal Adjustment", *Economic Policy* 13, no. 27, 1998: 489–545.

7 Carmen M. Reinhart and Kenneth S. Rogoff, "Growth in a Time of Debt", *National Bureau of Economic Research* (Working Paper 15639, 2010).
8 Alberto Alesina, Roberto Perotti, Jose Tavares, Maurice Obstfeld, and Barry Eichengreen, "The Political Economy of Fiscal Adjustments", *Brookings Papers on Economic Activity*, 1998, 213.
9 "Why Does Michael Gove Keep Referring to the Blob?", *The Guardian*, 2 October 2013.
10 Henry Mance, "Britain Has Had Enough of Experts, Says Gove", *Financial Times*, 3 June 2016.
11 There's a wealth of data on the Office for National Statistics (ONS) website; for strike days see https://www.ons.gov.uk/employmentandlabourmarket/p eopleinwork/employmentandemployeetypes/timeseries/f8xz/lms.
12 Katy Austin and Kate Whannel, "Rishi Sunak Disappointed New Rail Strike Law Not Used, Says No 10", *BBC News*, 29 January 2024, https://www.bbc. co.uk/news/uk-politics-68131541 (accessed 28 February 2024).
13 "Official Statistics, Rough Sleeping Snapshot in England: Autumn 2020", Ministry of Housing, Communities and Local Government, 25 February 2020, https://www.gov.uk/government/statistics/rough-sleeping-snapshot-i n-england-autumn-2020/rough-sleeping-snapshot-in-england-autumn-2020 (accessed 28 February 2024).
14 Matthew Keep, "The Budget Deficit: A Short Guide", House of Commons Library, 15 January 2024.
15 A useful source for all kinds of measures of household debt can be found at: https://www.statista.com/topics/10449/personal-debt-in-the-uk/#top icOverview.
16 For savings see Bee Boileau, Jonathan Cribb, and Thomas Wernham, "Characteristics and Consequences of Families with Low Levels of Financial Wealth", *Institute for Fiscal Studies*, June 2023.
17 You can follow Wren-Lewis's blog, 'Mainly Macro', at: https://mainlyma cro.blogspot.com/.
18 For productivity figures see Daniel Harari, "Productivity: Key Economic Indicators", House of Commons Library, 16 February 2024, https://comm onslibrary.parliament.uk/research-briefings/sn02791/ (accessed 2 April 2024).
19 For the operation of government debt and why it isn't like a household see Stephanie Kelton, *The Deficit Myth: Modern Monetary Theory and How to Build a Better Economy* (London, John Murray, 2020), particularly chapter 1.
20 Thomas Herndon, Michael Ash, and Robert Pollin, "Does High Public Debt Consistently Stifle Economic Growth? A Critique of Reinhart and Rogoff", *Political Economy Research Institute Working Paper Series* no. 322, April 2013.
21 Paul Krugman, *Arguing with Zombies: Economics, Politics and the Fight for a Better Future* (New York, W. W. Norton and Company, 2020), 185.
22 See John McDonnell, *Economics for the Many* (London, Verso, 2018).

References

"Official Statistics, Rough Sleeping Snapshot in England: Autumn 2020", Ministry of Housing, Communities and Local Government, 25 February 2020, https://www.gov.uk/government/statistics/rough-sleeping-snapshot-in-england-autumn-2020/rough-sleeping-snapshot-in-england-autumn-2020 (accessed 28 February 2024).

"Universal Credit: Welfare that Works", Department for Work and Pensions (Cm 7957, 2010).

"Why Does Michael Gove Keep Referring to the Blob?", *The Guardian*, 2 October 2013.

Alesina, A. and Ardagna, S. "Tales of Fiscal Adjustment", *Economic Policy* 13, no. 27, 1998: 489–545.

Alesina, A., Perotti, R., Tavares, J., Obstfeld, M., and Eichengreen, B. "The Political Economy of Fiscal Adjustments", *Brookings Papers on Economic Activity*, 1998.

Austin, K. and Whannel, K. "Rishi Sunak Disappointed New Rail Strike Law Not Used, Says No 10", *BBC News*, 29 January 2024, https://www.bbc.co.uk/news/uk-politics-68131541 (accessed 28 February 2024).

Blyth, M. *Austerity: The History of a Dangerous Idea* (Oxford, Oxford University Press, 2018).

Boileau, B., Cribb, J., and Wernham, T. "Characteristics and Consequences of Families with Low Levels of Financial Wealth", Institute for Fiscal Studies, June 2023.

Byrne, L. "'I'm Afraid There is no Money'. The Letter I Will Regret For Ever", *The Guardian*, 9 May 2015.

Harari, D. "Productivity: Key Economic Indicators", House of Commons Library, 16 February 2024, https://commonslibrary.parliament.uk/research-briefings/sn02791/ (accessed 2 April 2024).

Herndon, T., Ash, M., and Pollin, R. "Does High Public Debt Consistently Stifle Economic Growth? A Critique of Reinhart and Rogoff", Political Economy Research Institute Working Paper Series no. 322, April 2013.

Keep, M. "The Budget Deficit: A Short Guide", House of Commons Library, 15 January 2024.

Kelton, S. *The Deficit Myth: Modern Monetary Theory and How to Build a Better Economy* (London, John Murray, 2020).

Mance, H. "Britain Has Had Enough of Experts, Says Gove", *Financial Times*, 3 June 2016.

Reinhart, C. and Rogoff, K. S. "Growth in a Time of Debt", National Bureau of Economic Research, Working Paper 15639, 2010.

Wren-Lewis, S. *The Lies we were Told: Politics, Economics, Austerity and Brexit* (Bristol, Bristol University Press, 2018).

13

'WHY DID NO ONE SEE IT COMING?'

When Queen Elizabeth II visited the London School of Economics in 2008, she opened a new building and did the usual pleasantries with the various university worthies who gathered to talk to her. During a conversation about the recent financial crisis the Queen asked a disarming, yet difficult question, 'Why did no one see it coming?'[1] The question was a slightly misleading one. In fact, there had been people who predicted the crisis coming, but most of them were not economists. The Queen's question is one which economics is still struggling with today.[2]

Perhaps Keynes explained the difficulty in answering the Queen's question when he wrote, 'economics assumptions are seldom or never satisfied, with the result that it cannot solve the economic problems of the actual world.'[3] Central to the ideas we've seen throughout this book are the concepts of perfect market information, the rational economic agent, and efficient markets. In this chapter, we focus on the actual world and outline why the assumptions that economists make fail to help us to understand that world.

Broken Models

Keynes considered himself a political economist, which meant that he was concerned to use economics as a tool for the benefit of society by placing the economy in its wider political context. We have seen that he

DOI: 10.4324/9781003161950-13

applied himself to practical problems during the First and Second World Wars, and in his writing he was keen to highlight how the very real problems people faced, particularly during the 1930s, might be remedied. By contrast, modern economics concerns itself with modelling theoretical economies.[4] When economics does turn its attention to real-world problems, bizarre outcomes can occur – as we will see in this chapter.

We saw in Chapter One that part of the problem of theoretically modelling economies is people. In theory, markets are efficient. They act to allocate scarce resources to where people want them, at a price they are prepared to pay. And that price itself is dictated by the so-called laws of supply and demand. If the cost of goods or a service is higher than what people are willing to pay, then eventually the price will decrease or the goods or service will no longer be offered. Likewise, if too many people are chasing after something in short supply, its price will increase. Markets are predicted to revert to equilibrium, with goods and services being bought and sold in quantities people want and at prices which people are willing to pay. Yet the seamless movement of prices towards equilibrium, which works well on a graph, does not work so well in reality. We saw in Chapter Five the idea that wages are 'sticky'. In a downturn they do not reduce quickly, particularly if there are strong trade unions resisting employers' attempts to pay workers less. (We also saw that this was one reason why neoliberal economists have argued in favour of the curtailment of trade unions, see Chapter Seven.) It is not just wages that are sticky, but prices too. Prices are rarely in a state of constant fluctuation. One study found that a typical product's price changes only 1.4 times a year and that most firms only undertake price reviews annually.[5] Markets simply don't work in practice as they do in theory.

How do economists defend themselves against these obvious flaws in theory that are often exposed by reality? The answer lies right back in the principles of classical economics, which we saw in Chapter Two. You'll remember that Adam Smith argued that economies work at their best when they are operated according to the 'invisible hand' of the market. And for the market to work properly, Smith argued that the 'visible hand' of the state needs to refrain from interfering in the economy in all but a small number of ways (such as protecting private property). Smith's argument was that to interfere with the market was to introduce the possibility of inefficiencies. This, as we saw in Chapters

Seven and Nine, was how neoliberal economics sought to justify privatisations and how, at every turn, social democracy was dismantled on
the basis that the state was run by self-interested politicians and
bureaucrats whose lack of profit motive made them inefficient at running organisations, or, worse still, gave them private sources of wealth.
This view was behind the argument that the 2007–2008 financial crisis
would have been avoided had there been less regulation, not more (see
Chapter Twelve for austerity and the further dismantling of social
democracy). Economics employs a similar reasoning for the failure of its
models – what it calls 'exogenous shocks'. A few years after the Queen's
visit to the London School of Economics, she toured the Bank of England. Once again, after chit-chat with notables, the conversation turned
to the causes of the financial crisis. One explanation given was that the
crisis had been more like an earthquake or another form of natural
disaster.[6] The Queen was given other reasons as to the crash, which, in
fairness, did include a lack of regulation and a confession that the
interconnectedness of financial markets had been underestimated. In
conversation, the Queen stated a belief that 'things had got a bit lax'. In
effect, this was two pillars of the British establishment shrugging their
shoulders and saying, 'Who would have thunk?' But as we saw in
Chapter Eleven, the causes of the financial crisis were laid down many
years before the crash, and the ideas that had given rise to those causes,
such as deregulation, were decades old.

The idea that interconnected economies were too complex to understand does deserve some attention. When we have been looking at the
laws of supply and demand, we have seen that the model used involves
two people: a buyer and a seller. Even when Hayek made his argument
about the millions and billions of transactions in the market being a
referendum on prices, all he was really doing was imagining millions
and billions of buyers and sellers. But we've seen that markets are distinctly more complex than that, and the fundamental models of economics struggling with this can lead to faulty assumptions on policy.
For example, in the six-month period in 2015 when Yanis Varoufakis
was the Greek Finance Minister (see Chapter Eight), he was under
pressure from the Troika's economic advisers to increase the Greek
state's revenue. Varoufakis became frustrated about the way in which
their models did not produce policies that could possibly work. To
prove his point, he asked the economic advisors to model what would
happen if Value Added Tax were to be increased from 23% to 223%.[7]

The model predicted that there would be a significant increase in the amount of tax revenue. But, having got this far through the book, you are, quite rightly, probably thinking that what would really happen would be a collapse in demand as prices became utterly unaffordable and, as a knock-on effect, a drop in tax revenues. Not to mention economic Armageddon.

The other issue with the modelling of supply and demand, which is also ignored in the teaching of economics, is that the model always reverts to equilibrium. In other words, there isn't a possibility for there not to be an equilibrium. That markets might not revert to equilibrium certainly does happen. We saw at length in Chapter Four examples of where this has been the case in the labour market, and hence why unemployment can persist in ways which the basic ideas of mainstream economics do not accept. This brings us back to Keynes, demand creation, and full employment. Yet, Keynes' ideas have, for the past 40 years or so, largely been dismissed by economists. Around the time of the monetarist turn in economic thinking, 1980, Robert Lucas wrote, 'At research seminars, people don't take Keynesian theorising seriously anymore; the audience starts to whisper and giggle to one another.'[8] As we saw in Chapter Twelve, Keynes had the last laugh as the financial crisis, and then Covid hit. But as we also saw, even then Lucas was not convinced that a return to Keynes' ideas was needed – 'but I don't think we are there yet' – and little has changed since. Given that we were on the back of the worst financial crisis in 90 years, and the worst pandemic in a hundred, you wonder what must happen to make mainstream economics reconsider its focus on free market, small-state economic ideas.

Our Problems Unfaced by Economics

In March 2011, Lord Kalms wrote to the *Times* outlining that years earlier he had offered to give a grant of £1 million to the London School of Economics to establish a professorship in Business Ethics. Whilst the director of the School was encouraging, the staff themselves rejected the offer 'as it saw no correlation between ethics and economics'.[9] This makes sense if you start from the position that the rational economic agent always acts to maximise their income. But it is quite some distance away even from the classical economists. John Stuart Mill wrote about the need to produce the 'greatest good for the greatest number'.[10]

By contrast, Friedman argued that, 'the only corporate social responsibility a corporation has is to maximise profits for its stockholders.'[11] He argued that as shareholders expect their money to be used to return a maximum profit, diverting resources away from that goal is fraud. Friedman's position doesn't give much room for non-market considerations and whilst firms might engage in a wider vision of corporate social responsibility, that vision has yet to permeate mainstream economics.

Of course, it might be OK to not worry too much about ethics if the economy worked in a way that satisfied the greatest number of people. However, increasingly wealth is becoming concentrated in the hands of a smaller (and shrinking) number of people. A 2014 report by Oxfam found that the 85 richest people in the world own the same amount of wealth as the 3.5 billion poorest people.[12] A trite position might be that those 85 people have worked hard to gain their just rewards and that the poorest in society are lazy. But it's not as though hard work is paying off like it used to. Since around 1980, we have seen a decoupling of wages and productivity. In the years of social democracy, as productivity increased so too did wages. This meant that productivity increased 119% in the US between 1947 and 1979, and wages increased 72% in the same period. But in the 20 years from 1979, productivity increased 80% whilst wages grew only 7%.[13] Marx may well have had a point; the increased wealth created was certainly going somewhere other than to workers.

One of the things about a market economy is that people need to be able to access the market in the first place. People in the US, Britain, and Europe, for example, have access to many of the markets that they want to access. It's worth considering that for a lot of people this isn't the case. Women in the Western world have been able to access labour markets in much greater numbers since the introduction of the contraceptive pill in the 1960s. But globally, such access is uneven, weakening women's ability to enter the labour market. Even where women can access the labour market, they are more likely to be in precarious work that is less well paid than that of their male counterparts, a factor which is a motive for women to withdraw from the labour market. And much of the domestic labour, which disproportionately falls on women, goes unrecompensed financially and is invisible in the usual measures of economic growth such as Gross Domestic Product. A vision of value that excludes much of our day-to-day essential tasks, and even the continuation of humanity, is unable to capture what being human is, yet economics pushes that to the sidelines.

It is not only current problems in the economy that pose a problem for economics, but future problems too. Records relating to climate are, in a bad way, being broken. In recent times, we have seen the warmest summer day on record in the UK; record melting of polar icecaps; and the warmest summer sea temperatures on record. The evidence of our eyes tells us that our climate is changing, and the scientific evidence strongly points to the idea that this is due to the output of carbon dioxide and other gasses from industrial production. It's not just that in the future the earth will be potentially less hospitable, or inhospitable, to humanity. Microplastics, linked to respiratory illness and cancer, are now being found in drinking water, and even in clouds lying atop the Himalayan mountains.[14] In Britain, our industrial and domestic output of waste water is so badly managed that our rivers and seas are being flooded with raw sewerage. Our environment is suffering because we are pursuing the idea that continued economic growth – the production of goods and services – is the route to greater prosperity for all, as we saw in Chapter Two. Smith may have believed that the role of the state is to provide common goods that are not in the interest of one entrepreneur to provide. Yet, the most concerted effort to remodel the British economy around a greener economy struggled to get traction, as we saw in Chapter Twelve. Mainstream economists have only interpreted a partial reconstruction of the world, often in mathematical ways. What they seem unable to do is change it.

Academic Economics as a Profession

In 2011, a group of economics students at Harvard University walked out of their class, handing the professor, Greg Mankiw, a letter in which the students protested at being offered supply and demand economics as the only basis for understanding the basic architecture of the academic Economics discipline.[15] The students wrote of their concern that the validity of the basic models used to underpin Economics was not critiqued as part of their study. In the wake of the 2007–2008 financial crisis, and during the 'Occupy Wall Street' protests of 2011, the students felt that, 'If Harvard fails to equip its students with a broad and critical understanding of economics, their actions are likely to harm the global financial system. The last five years of economic turmoil have been proof of this.'[16] Questioning professors at Harvard looks like revolutionary stuff to Harvard professors, and in fairness questioning them in an incredibly hierarchical discipline such as Economics looks even more so. But in truth, the protest, which sparked off counter-protests from more mainstream-minded economics students and which prompted Mankiw to respond to his students in the letter pages of *The New York Times*, amounted to not much more than wanting to be taught a bit of Keynes.[17] Self-confessedly, the protesters' concerns had not so much to do with changing the global economy but, rather, preventing another catastrophe within it.

It was not long, though, before the contagion of questioning the Economics curriculum spread. In 2013, at the University of Manchester, students protested the way in which academic Economics taught to them had continued to rely on free market principles, even though the problems with an excess of these had been laid bare by the 2007–2008 financial crisis.[18] Not only calling for Keynes to feature on the curriculum, they also called for their studies to include Marx as well – a call which, to an Economics department, probably did look like a full-blown revolution. These students gained traction in the national press and went on to establish the Post-Crash Economics Society to press their case. As one third-year student put it, given the focus on mathematics and models in Economics, students tend to avoid subjects which require reading or essay writing and in which economic ideas are contested, such as history of economic thought or economic and business history. As a result of focussing on mainstream economic ideas, they wrote, 'students never develop the faculties necessary to critically question, evaluate and compare economic theories, and enter the working world with a false belief about what economics is.'[19] Perhaps they should have said 'what economics should be'.

The launch of the Post-Crash Economics Society at Manchester caused quite a stir. In parliament, MPs including Jeremy Corbyn and John MacDonald tabled a motion in support of the questioning of a 'free market model [that] has resulted in a massive increase in wealth for the richest one per cent of the population, whilst the vast majority of people have seen their incomes, terms of employment, public services, and standard of living eroded'.[20] But at Manchester, the university pushed back against the Post-Crash Economics Society. The head of Economics likened non-mainstream (heterodox) economics to quack medicine. Another professor in the department conceded that some change was required in the light of the crash, but held that micro-economics, where, as we have seen, many free market ideas come from, was 'robust' and that it was macro-economics, the economics inspired by Keynes, that was 'broken'. The department conceded to an after-hours, non-credit-bearing module being provided. But once set up and taught for one year, it was rejected as a module in the department's curriculum. Not long after, the temporary lecturer who taught the module was forced to seek work elsewhere.

Whilst it is true that there were staff in Economics at Manchester who could have taught Marx to the department's students, that the department might tolerate such a thing was unlikely. Part of the reason for that lies in the history of the University of Manchester. Established in the nineteenth century, the university has traditionally been business facing. And Manchester was the heartland of the move against protectionism in the form of the Navigation Acts and the Corn Laws, as we saw in Chapters Two and Eight. But in larger part, the answers as to why Economics more generally has been so slow to challenge mainstream economic ideas may well lie in the staffing of Economics departments. For example, it is not much of a surprise that women's voices are poorly represented in Economics. Women from the UK make up only 27% of Economics undergraduates (and overall women only make up 32% of Economics undergraduates), whilst only 26% of academic staff are women. Only 15% of professors are women. Between 2012 and 2019 there was not a single black professor of Economics employed in the whole of the UK.[21] Only three women have won the Nobel Prize in Economics, around 2% of the total. It was as late as 2023 that a Nobel was awarded for work on women in the economy. Overall, Economics is a very male-dominated academic discipline. It also has a core of around five top journals, publication in which is essential for promotion, meaning that economists' work tends towards the orthodox norms of those journals.

Conclusion

And yet...

Perhaps surprisingly, not everyone in the economics world approved of the University of Manchester's resistance to questioning mainstream economics. Some economists such as Joseph Stiglitz supported the idea of a new, more critical, module, and even the then Governor of the

Bank of England, Andy Haldane, showed support. More broadly, in their study of the economics Nobel Prize, *The Nobel Factor*, Avner Offer and Gabriel Soderberg explore the effects of the Nobel on the economics profession.[22] They note that the Nobel Prize recognises that outside the mainstream of economics teaching, there are economists whose research is consistent with free market thinking, and economists who favour social democratic ideas. In order not to appear partisan to either side (and therefore undermine the desire to win the prize), the Nobel awarding committee tends to pretty much award equally to both free market and social democratic economists. Yet when surveyed, Offer and Soderberg noted that roughly two-thirds of economists tend to favour social democratic solutions to economic problems. In other words, the Nobel distorts the importance of free market economics amongst economists. This leaves the obvious question as to why it is that the free market ideas we have seen throughout this book have found favour as ideas underpinning government policy when they are not particularly favoured by economists personally. We turn to this in the next, our final, chapter.

Notes

1 Rupert Neate, "Queen Finally Finds out Why no One Saw the Financial Crisis Coming", *The Guardian*, 13 December 2012.
2 For example, James Fulcher, *Capitalism: A Very Short Introduction* (Oxford, Oxford University Press, 2004) concludes by speculating on a forthcoming large financial crisis.
3 Keynes expands on this in his concluding notes to the General Theory, John Maynard Keynes, *The General Theory of Employment, Interest and Money* (London, BN Publishing, 2008), chapter 24.
4 For the problems of economic models see Robert Skidelsky, *What's Wrong with Economics?: A Guide for the Perplexed* (New Haven, Yale University Press, 2021), chapter 5.
5 Alan S. Blinder, Elie R. D. Canetti, David E. Lebow, and Jeremy B. Rudd, *Asking about Prices: A New Approach to Understanding Price Stickiness* (New York, Russell Sage Foundation, 1998).
6 Neate, "Queen Finally Finds out Why".
7 Yanis Varoufakis, *Adults in the Room: My Battle with Europe's Deep Establishment* (London, The Bodley Head, 2017), 417.
8 Paul Krugman, "Review, Keynes: The Return of the Master by Robert Skidelsky", *The Guardian*, 30 August 2009.
9 Lord Kalms, "Ethics Boys", Letter to *The Times*, 8 March 2011.
10 John Stuart Mill (edited by Roger Crisp), *Utilitarianism* (Oxford, Oxford University Press, 1998), 81.

11 Milton Friedman, "A Friedman Doctrine: The Social Responsibility of Business is to Increase Its Profits", *The New York Times Magazine*, 13 September 1970.
12 "Working for the Few: Political Capture and Economic Inequality", Oxfam Briefing Paper 178, 20 January 2014.
13 Robert Reich, "The State of Working America", *New York Times*, 4 September 2011.
14 Damian Carrington, "Microplastic Pollution Found near Summit of Mount Everest", *The Guardian*, 20 November 2020.
15 For an account from the group which formed out of this protest, see https://www.rethinkeconomics.org/about/.
16 Concerned Students of Economics 10, "An Open Letter to Greg Mankiw", *Harvard Political Review*, 2 November 2011, https://harvardpolitics.com/an-open-letter-to-greg-mankiw/ (accessed 29 February 2024).
17 N. Gregory Mankiw, "Know What You're Protesting", *New York Times*, 3 December 2011.
18 Phillip Inman, "Economics Students Aim to Tear up Free-Market Syllabus", *The Guardian*, 24 October 2013.
19 Ibid.
20 "Formation of the Post-Crash Economics Society at Manchester University", UK Parliament, Early Day Motions, EDM 641, 29 October 2013.
21 Victoria Bateman, Danula Kankanam Gamage, Erin Hengel, and Xianyue Liu, "The Gender Imbalance in UK Economics", *Royal Economic Society*, July 2021.
22 Avner Offer and Gabriel Soderberg, *The Nobel Factor: The Prize in Economics, Social Democracy and the Market Turn* (Princeton, New Jersey, Princeton University Press, 2016).

References

"Working for the Few: Political Capture and Economic Inequality", Oxfam Briefing Paper 178, 20 January 2014.
Bateman, V., Gamage, D. K., Hengel, E., and Liu, X. "The Gender Imbalance in UK Economics", Royal Economic Society, July 2021.
Blinder, A. S., Canetti, E. R. D., Lebow, D. E., and Rudd, J. B. *Asking about Prices: A New Approach to Understanding Price Stickiness* (New York, Russell Sage Foundation, 1998).
Carrington, D. "Microplastic Pollution Found near Summit of Mount Everest", *The Guardian*, 20 November 2020.
Concerned Students of Economics 10, "An Open Letter to Greg Mankiw", *Harvard Political Review*, 2 November 2011, https://harvardpolitics.com/an-open-letter-to-greg-mankiw/ (accessed 29 February 2024).
Fulcher, J. *Capitalism: A Very Short Introduction* (Oxford, Oxford University Press, 2004).
Friedman, M. "A Friedman Doctrine: The Social Responsibility of Business is to Increase Its Profits", *The New York Times Magazine*, 13 September 1970.

Inman, P. "Economics Students Aim to Tear up Free-Market Syllabus", *The Guardian*, 24 October 2013.

Kalms, Lord, "Ethics Boys", Letter to *The Times*, 8 March 2011.

Keynes, J. M. *The General Theory of Employment, Interest and Money* (London, BN Publishing, 2008).

Krugman, P. "Review, Keynes: The Return of the Master by Robert Skidelsky", *The Guardian*, 30 August 2009.

Mankiw, N. G. "Know What You're Protesting", *New York Times*, 3 December 2011.

Mill, J. S. (ed. R. Crisp). *Utilitarianism* (Oxford, Oxford University Press, 1998).

Neate, R. "Queen Finally Finds out Why no One Saw the Financial Crisis Coming", *The Guardian*, 13 December 2012.

Offer, A. and Soderberg, G. *The Nobel Factor: The Prize in Economics, Social Democracy and the Market Turn* (Princeton, New Jersey, Princeton University Press, 2016).

Reich, R. "The State of Working America", *New York Times*, 4 September 2011.

Skidelsky, R. *What's Wrong with Economics?: A Guide for the Perplexed* (New Haven, Yale University Press, 2021).

UK Parliament, Early Day Motions, "Formation of the Post-Crash Economics Society at Manchester University", EDM 641, 29 October 2013.

Varoufakis, Y. *Adults in the Room: My Battle with Europe's Deep Establishment* (London, The Bodley Head, 2017).

14

ECONOMICS OVERREACH

In 2022, the economist Ann Pettifor, author of several works calling for a Green New Deal, took to Twitter/X to delight in Andrew Lilico being introduced on BBC Radio 4 as a 'right-wing economist'.[1] Lilico, a columnist for the *Telegraph*, frequent collaborator with the Institute of Economic Affairs, and director of the economics consultancy firm Europe Economics, could well be described as right-wing. But to some, the description might look odd. On the one hand, many economists see their discipline as a science. It would not make sense for us to describe someone as a right-wing physicist because discovery in physics does not diverge on political lines. The focus of mainstream economics on mathematical modelling and its reluctance to talk across disciplines to the rest of the social sciences have helped it to defend its internal belief that economics is a science – as immune to political conflict as is physics.[2] On the other hand, those on the political left would consider it odd to describe economics as anything other than right-wing, politically speaking. But the situation is even more complicated than that. We have seen that economic ideas have been central to political debate for the past few hundred years and that many of these ideas have underpinned right-wing political thought. However, as we saw at the end of Chapter Thirteen, there are plenty of economists whose policy preferences are more in keeping with social democracy than neoliberalism.

It makes sense to ask why it is that the economic ideas that underpin right-wing politics have, in the last 40 years, posed such a formidable

DOI: 10.4324/9781003161950-14

challenge to social democratic ideas, especially as academic economists tend to have sympathy for social democratic ideas. Simon Wren-Lewis describes the problem as 'neoliberal overreach'.[3] His argument is that politicians have gone too far in exhorting the core principles of neoliberalism. So, on Brexit, Wren-Lewis argues that the neoliberal position on the European Union was that leaving would allow for a reduction in the size of the state and a more free market; these benefits of leaving would outweigh dislocation from Britain's largest neighbouring market. Wren-Lewis, who made strong economic arguments for Remain, argues that if the mainstream of the economics profession were more regularly featured in the news, then economic justifications for Brexit would have gained little traction. Instead, Wren-Lewis argues, the media features rent-a-gob economists, such as Lilico, and the founder of 'Economists for Brexit' Patrick Minford, who will happily go on programmes such as *Newsnight* and argue for slashing the size of the state or leaving the European Union.[4] In other words, Wren-Lewis argues that the mainstream media deny the public access to 'good' economics.

Wren-Lewis's argument is in part convincing. But we need to go further. It is not so much that we are seeing neoliberal overreach, but, rather, overreach by the economics profession as a whole which has focussed teaching and research in its departments largely on the mainstream, sidelining heterodox views. Economics' journey from moral philosophy, to political economics, to economics has isolated it from the political realm but it has not prevented politicians from picking and choosing economics ideas for their advantage. Economics' focus on mathematically modelling worlds of its own conceiving has diverted it away from a view of society as a whole.[5] Having surrendered the political ground in economic discussions, the vacuum has been filled by political ideologies that have used some of the fundamentals of mainstream economic thinking, such as the small state and self-interested entrepreneur, and presented them to the public as politically desirable and economically scientific objectives. In turn, this has set a political agenda focussed not on collective solutions to society's organisation and people's problems, but individualist ones. By reaching for truths of a perfectly modelled economic system, economics has enabled its core ideas to be perverted to justify the problems of our real world.

We saw in Chapter Nine that Thatcher's 1981 budget represented a turning point in post-war economic policy. It represented a moment in which Keynesian-inspired social democratic ideas fell to neoliberal ones.

The years following were no less critical. With the failure of monetarism, the Thatcher government's economic policy became less about following the ideas of academic economists and more about reconfiguring the economy around an individualist ethos. At its heart, mainstream economics is individualistic. We saw in Chapter Two Smith's argument that it is not from 'benevolence' that people produce the goods we need to sustain ourselves, but from a desire to make a profit. We also explored Smith's idea that by people seeking to maximise profit, everyone would benefit by Pareto Improvement – a state in which people can enrich themselves but not by harming others. If this model view of the world were true, then the individualism which economics has justified in our political system could still be of benefit to all. Yet we saw in Chapter Nine that this individualism in the housing market, particularly around social housing, has distorted the housing market into something other than what it should be – a way of distributing homes to those who need housing. Rather than helping the economy as a whole, the individual's right to own property as an investment, rather than as a home, or the right to remove housing from the social housing stock for use solely by them until sold, has created a situation where entering the housing market is impossible for many. It has also swollen the costs of rents. The problem is not just that housing is unaffordable or expensive for some people, whilst being luxurious to others. It is also that the housing market pits individuals against each other. We saw in Chapter Nine that high interest rates are hard for those with mortgages, whilst those living with savings benefit from higher rates. Meanwhile, those with savings want to see low inflation and the use of higher interest rates to reduce those rates, a policy that is designed to create unemployment.

Instead of people striving to improve themselves and inadvertently benefiting those around them, they strive to improve themselves but are pitted against others. In the housing market we see the tensions between young and old; homeowners, mortgage payers, and 'generation rent'; and those with savings and the unemployed. Housing is one way to get into the problem that economic individualism creates, but it is one that is replicated across the economy. We see these tensions everywhere: the in-work who resent supporting those without work; the educated person who derides the school dropout; the healthy person who resents the cost of caring for the chronically ill or the recipient of a free prescription; the out-of-work person who resents a migrant with a job; the ratepayer whose contempt for the homeless person is tinged with a fear of what could be. And in the end, a fortress mentality. Build the wall or send back the boats. 'Send them to Rwanda and show strength,' as the Tory Party Vice-Chairman put it when he proposed a breach of the rule of law after the Supreme Court ruled Suella Braverman's so-called 'Rwanda' plan unlawful – an act somewhat akin to capitalism's head proposing to eat its own tail.[6]

A Ministry of Common Sense

In his 2023 Cabinet reshuffle, Prime Minister Rishi Sunak created a 'Ministry for Common Sense' led by Esther McVey. McVey's appointment was intended to placate the far right of the Conservative Party who were dismayed after the sacking of Suella Braverman as Home Secretary. As part of an attempt to stoke fears of 'wokeness' in Britain and signal a need to legislate it away, it was a pretty representative act by a party which has almost completely lost any vestige of its 'one nation' beliefs. But could a ministry of economic common sense benefit politicians and the public?

Wren-Lewis argues that were more academic economists given greater coverage in the media then people would be armed with better information about the economy and be better able to support good policies and condemn bad ones, such as austerity. But the problem is more than just lack of access to 'good' economics. First, what Wren-Lewis really wants is not so much to get less partisan economics in the media but to get economics that comes from a macro perspective in it. We saw in Chapter Thirteen how the micro-focussed economists of the International Monetary Fund had little regard for issues of demand when they predicted that an increase in VAT from 23% to 223% would lead to a relative increase in tax revenue. Putting issues of demand to the fore in a crisis would certainly have advanced the debate over austerity in the run-up to the 2010 election. But the bigger problem we face is not so much that our society struggles to apply micro- and macroeconomic policy in the correct ways at the correct times, but that ideas that deviate from an individualistic understanding of society are drowned out, which prevents us from collectively solving problems. This is more than simply a question of which part of economic policy to implement and when. Wren-Lewis got a taste of this in response to his blogging on the continued inflation of 2023. Having called throughout the 2010s for government spending in response to the Great Recession,

Wren-Lewis was favoured by those on the political left. Such favour continued when, in response to the inflation caused by the Ukraine war, he advocated leaving interest rates low because he believed the inflation to be driven by war, something external to the British economy, and raising rates would therefore not only be unable to achieve a decrease in inflation but would also suppress demand and spark a further, deeper recession. But in 2023, Wren-Lewis came to believe that the inflation caused by the war had been replaced by inflation driven from within the British economy, not least of all by workers pressing for substantial pay rises to combat the cost-of-living crisis. Like a good macro-economist, he advised that rates should stay high to dampen demand in the UK economy and bring inflation down. At this point, he lost the support of the political left, who did not want to choose creating higher unemployment as a policy that would solve Britain's inflation problem. It was not so much that people wanted good economic advice, but rather that they wanted something that went beyond the standard economics. Something that would give them new tools, tools that would change society, not just bring it back to equilibrium.

Some economists have attempted to apply their work to radical policy development, such as Ann Pettifor's work on the Green New Deal. But politically, Pettifor's plan got little traction because it became associated with the Labour Party under Jeremy Corbyn, who pledged to implement the Green New Deal in the party's 2019 election manifesto. Corbyn's manifesto was radical by the standards of today, though much of its content didn't look much different from the ideas parties had put forward in the social democratic age, pre-neoliberalism. Despite presenting a vision of a future Britain based around good clean energy, jobs that would benefit not only the environment but also people, and the prospect of families saving money by living in energy-efficient homes, the plan gained little traction. Even when Keir Starmer's leadership adopted the idea for a Green New Deal, it was attacked by the Institute for Economic Affairs for privileging a small number of workers with well-paying jobs 'at the expense of real jobs for the many'. The implication being that government would be misdirecting investment at the cost of jobs created by the application of market forces. In the end, Starmer all but abandoned the idea.

Worse still, the Green New Deal put green economic policies into the public domain in such a way that proponents could get targeted by the anti-'woke' politics of the Conservative Party that grew in strength after the resignation of Boris Johnson as Prime Minister. In 2023, Sunak abolished policies designed to get Britain to net zero carbon emissions by 2050. In a move that would please oil barons and petrolhead motorists equally, Sunak delayed the banning of internal combustion engines from 2030 to 2035. In relation to the abolition of gas boilers for heating, Sunak delayed this by nine years, citing the language of the individual's right to purchase what they want to in a free market. 'We will never force anyone to rip out their existing boiler and replace it with a heat pump.' In truth, no one was proposing that government officials come to people's houses and rip out their boiler. It was simply about making the available technology greener. Alongside announcing other U-turns, the policy announcement took a particularly silly tone when Sunak promised to abolish plans for households to have seven bins for different types of waste, despite such a plan not existing. The *Daily Mail* characterised Sunak's policy change as 'lashing out at ideological eco-zealots who don't care about families'.[7]

Pettifor is a well-respected economist. But it is hard to see how heterodox economics is going to manage to get past the individualist attitude which mainstream economics has instilled in public political thought. Worse still, this thinking has seeped out into the most niche and extreme ideas. The rise in men considering themselves as involuntarily celibate, abbreviated to 'Incel', is a global phenomenon particularly found in North America and organised both in, and against, social media. A 2021 paper by Preston, Halpin, and Maguire found that Incels organised around the ideas that women were using dating apps to 'marry up'; that dating apps allowed 'highly desirable men... to partner with multiple women'; and that social media allowed 'subordinate men' to 'inflate women's egos and their "sexual marketplace value"'. The dating equivalent of a vision of a distorted marketplace might seem obtuse, but a string of attacks perpetrated on women by Incels demonstrates that ideas taken from mainstream economics are having very real and grave consequences outside of the economic realm.[8]

Political Overreach

When Liz Truss launched her disastrous 2022 budget, it ended one of the shortest terms of office in history for a British Prime Minister. The budget was based on growing the economy by slashing tax in the hope that this would encourage entrepreneurial activity. But the way in which she proposed to cover the cost, by borrowing to fund a tax cut for the rich, spooked the financial markets, sending the value of the pound into a downward spiral. Mortgage lenders anticipated that the Bank of England would have to raise interest rates, which led to the withdrawal of hundreds of mortgage products from the market because lenders anticipated an increase in mortgage repayment rates. Final salary pension schemes saw the value of government debt decrease and given that they rely heavily on government debt to fund themselves, this put schemes, and people's pensions, in considerable jeopardy. It would be easy enough to see the reasons for this disastrous budget lying in class interest – the Conservative party giving money to their supporters before an election and asking the broader populace to pay for it through debt. There's some truth in that; after all, the Sunak government, which followed Truss's, toyed seriously with abolishing inheritance tax, something which would do nothing for the economy at large but which would benefit rich people located largely in the South East of England. But, after Truss's government fell, her protests about the way in which her budget was received suggest she had some genuine belief in her proposed policies. Truss argued:

> Some say this is a crisis of capitalism – that free markets are responsible. But that is not borne out by the facts. Quite the opposite is true. The fact is that since the Labour government was elected in 1997, we have moved towards being a more corporatist social democracy in Britain than we were in the 1980s and 1990s.[9]

Truss's appeal to furthering the cause of the spirited free market individual over the collective efforts of social democracy fits with many of the free market ideas we have seen throughout this book. The problem is that Truss's analysis does not fit with reality. Far from New Labour reviving social democracy, the Blair and Brown governments finally nailed down neoliberal economic policies in the British economy and did so in such a way that later attempts to shift the Labour Party back to a social democratic position failed. The failure of Truss's policies could not solely be explained by a fantasy of the resurrection of social democracy. Truss then claimed to have been undermined by an economic establishment (in the form of the Treasury, Bank of England, and Office for Budget Responsibility) that had succumbed to 'an orthodoxy that was gradually moving to the left'.[10] When we place the idea of left-wing economists undermining free market policies in the context of the ideas we have seen throughout this book – not least of all the hostility to even a bit of basic Keynesianism in the Economics curriculum which we saw in Chapter Thirteen – Truss's claim seems laughable.

The Ideas That Rule Us

It is hard to see how any solutions to the growing list of problems society faces will come from within the economics profession. The ideas that underpin mainstream economics have been used to reinforce the political decisions made in the management of our economic affairs. They have been used to justify the gender pay gap; inaction on climate change; the underfunding and privatisation of public services; homelessness; and reduction of support for the unemployed, to name but a few. A pure model of the economy, even if it could be achieved, cannot rectify these issues because they are not only economic issues but also moral, ethical, philosophical, and political ones. The further our understanding of 'the economy' (a concept that is relatively recent) has moved away from political economy and moral philosophy, the less able has mainstream economics been to solve the challenges which we face. And there is little sign of real appetite to move economics back into the realm of political economy. It is questionable as to whether such a move is now possible, with those interventions by economists into political life, such as proposals around the Green New Deal, faltering because of the broader public's doubts about what it is possible to achieve.

Just as it is hard to see how the economics profession can provide us with innovative ideas to help us begin to fix the economic problems of society, it is hard to see how the application of economics ideas by politicians can do so either. The 'third way' did not create a new space in which the excesses of capitalism or Soviet state planning could be avoided. Instead, it entrenched the neoliberal ideas that had been growing in common currency since the end of the Second World War and implemented from the late 1970s onwards. What is considered possible is limited by an individualistic conception of the economy which accepts inequality and encourages people to put themselves first. Yet even the super-rich are slowly coming to accept that this is no way to run society. In the run-up to the Treasury's 2023 Autumn Statement, a group of 'Patriotic Millionaires' projected a message onto the Bank of England that read 'Tax Our Wealth'. The group released a statement saying, 'For a better Britain our government should prioritise taxing those of us who can most afford it.'[11]

If a consensus might be emerging that taxing the rich more to help society could be a good idea, we would have to return to the question of what such help would look like. It is worth remembering that whilst it was Keynes's belief in state planning that provided economic justifications for social democracy, it was Beveridge's priorities in tackling the 'Five Giants' that set out what social democracy would look like in practice in Britain. Education, decent housing, access to health care, assistance for the unemployed and people with disabilities, and the ability to feed and shelter ourselves affordably are still worthwhile goals. Keynes believed that by around 2030, we would be able to provide these basics with such effortlessness that we would have to start a new discussion as to what to do with all our spare time. Sadly, he has been proved wrong, though, for better or for worse, the development of artificial intelligence may make such a discussion pertinent in the not-too-distant future. For the time being, we need to recognise that in our society, the individualism which mainstream economics has promoted has been used to justify the petty small-mindedness of the anti-'woke' brigade and our collective lack of action to support those worse off than ourselves. But we strived for better in the era of social democracy, and whilst those ideas, in the form they took at that time, are of their time, that does not stop us from applying their basic principles to the creation of a more equal society in future. This will require us to debate what our future society should look like, how it should be organised, and how it is funded. For there to be genuine innovation, it will require us to be able to spot the ideas that, at present, rule us.

Notes

1 "BBC World at One" (@AnnPettifor, 28 September 2022).
2 Even economic history, traditionally firmly part of the Economics curriculum, now treats history as a potential source of new data to apply models to, rather than an analytical tool or narrative device; see Robert Skidelsky, *What's Wrong with Economics?: A Guide for the Perplexed* (New Haven, Yale University Press, 2021), chapter 11.
3 Simon Wren-Lewis, *The Lies we were Told: Politics, Economics, Austerity and Brexit* (Bristol, Bristol University Press, 2018), 267–274.
4 See Wren-Lewis, *The Lies we were Told* for an analysis of what he calls 'media macro' – the way in which the media discusses the economy as a whole. Wren-Lewis argues, convincingly, that it is the press that offers forward as legitimate economic ideas based upon individualism and which consistently peddles myths such as the supposed need for austerity in 2010.
5 See Ben Fine, "Economic Imperialism and Intellectual Progress: The Present as History of Economic Thought?", *History of Economics Review* 32, no. 1,

2016: 10–35 for an analysis of the journey from political economy to economics and for an analysis of how, when economics does now speak to other social science disciplines, it does so by imposing the self-interested economic agent on the world views of those disciplines.

6 Rajeev Syal, "What Options are Left for Rishi Sunak after Supreme Court's Rwanda Ruling?", *The Guardian*, 15 November 2023.

7 David Wilcock and Jason Groves, "Rishi Sunak Lashes out at 'Ideological' Eco-Zealots Who 'Don't Care about Families' as he Comes out Swinging to Defend Green U-Turn Saying Brits Should not be Hit with £15,000 Cost of New Cars, Boilers and Eco-Taxes Earlier than the Rest of the World", *Daily Mail*, 21 September 2023.

8 Kayla Preston, Michael Halpin, and Finlay Maguire, "The Black Pill: New Technology and the Male Supremacy of Involuntarily Celibate Men", *Men and Masculinities* 24, no. 5, 2021: 832–841.

9 Kiran Stacey, "Liz Truss: Economic Consensus since 1997 to Blame for UK Woes – Not Me", *The Guardian*, 17 September 2023.

10 Ibid.

11 Rupert Neate, "UK Millionaires Group Projects 'Tax our Wealth' on to Treasury and Bank of England", *The Guardian*, 21 November 2023.

References

Fine, B. "Economic Imperialism and Intellectual Progress: The Present as History of Economic Thought?", *History of Economics Review* 32, no. 1, 2016: 10–35.

Neate, R. "UK Millionaires Group Projects 'Tax our Wealth' on to Treasury and Bank of England", *The Guardian*, 21 November 2023.

Preston, K., Halpin, M., and Maguire, F. "The Black Pill: New Technology and the Male Supremacy of Involuntarily Celibate Men", *Men and Masculinities* 24, no. 5, 2021: 832–841.

Skidelsky, R. *What's Wrong with Economics?: A Guide for the Perplexed* (New Haven, Yale University Press, 2021).

Stacey, K. "Liz Truss: Economic Consensus since 1997 to Blame for UK Woes – Not Me", *The Guardian*, 17 September 2023.

Syal, R. "What Options are Left for Rishi Sunak after Supreme Court's Rwanda Ruling?", *The Guardian*, 15 November 2023.

Wilcock, D. and Groves, J. "Rishi Sunak Lashes out at 'Ideological' Eco-Zealots who 'Don't Care about Families' as he Comes out Swinging to Defend Green U-turn Saying Brits Should not be Hit with £15,000 Cost of New Cars, Boilers and Eco-Taxes Earlier than the Rest of the World", *Daily Mail*, 21 September 2023 (accessed 4 April 2024).

Wren-Lewis, S. *The Lies we were Told: Politics, Economics, Austerity and Brexit* (Bristol, Bristol University Press, 2018).

BIBLIOGRAPHY

"A Safe Bet for Success – Modernising Britain's Gambling Laws", Department for Culture, Media and Sport (London, HMSO, 26 March 2002).

"Changes in the Value and Division of Unpaid Care Work in the UK: 2000–2015", Office of National Statistics, 10 November 2016, https://www.ons.gov.uk/economy/nationalaccounts/satelliteaccounts/articles/changesinthevalueanddivision ofunpaidcareworkintheuk/2000to2015#:~:text=In%202015%2C%20mothers%2 0spent%2C%20on,total%20childcare%20time%20in%202015 (accessed 21 February 2024).

"Energy Pricing and the Future of the Energy Market", House of Commons, Business, Energy and Industrial Strategy Committee, 19 July 2022.

"Mick Lynch Explains a Picket Line to Kay Burley", 26 July 2022, https://www.youtube.com/watch?v=HufDB6QDXTc (accessed 21 February 2024).

"Official Statistics, Rough Sleeping Snapshot in England: Autumn 2020", Ministry of Housing, Communities and Local Government, 25 February 2020, https://www.gov.uk/government/statistics/rough-sleeping-snapshot-in-england -autumn-2020/rough-sleeping-snapshot-in-england-autumn-2020 (accessed 28 February 2024).

"RMT General Secretary Mick Lynch Quizzed on Whether He's a Marxist amid Biggest Rail Strike", *Good Morning Britain*, 21 June 2022, https://www.youtube.com/watch?v=QB4M4ugvaVg (accessed 21 February 2024).

"The Government's Proposals for Gambling: Nothing to Lose", Department for Culture, Media and Sport (London, HMSO, 17 July 2002).

"The Scale of Economic Inequality in the UK", The Equality Trust, 2022, https://equalitytrust.org.uk/scale-economic-inequality-uk#:~:text=Worldwide%

2C%20the%20top%200.01%25%20owned,increase%20in%20wealth%20for
%20billionaires.&text=The%20graph%20below%20shows%20how%20wea
lth%20distribution%20has%20changed%20since,held%20the%20majority%
20of%20wealth (accessed 21 February 2024).

"Tony Blair: 'My Job was to Build on Some Thatcher Policies'", *BBC News*, 8
April 2013, https://www.bbc.co.uk/news/av/uk-politics-22073434 (accessed 27
March 2024).

"Train Derailment at Hatfield: A Final Report by the Independent Investigation
Board" (London, Office of Rail Regulation, July 2006), https://www.railwaysa
rchive.co.uk/documents/HSE_HatfieldFinal2006.pdf (accessed 4 April 2024).

"Universal Credit: Welfare that Works", Department for Work and Pensions
(Cm 7957, 2010).

"Why Does Michael Gove Keep Referring to the Blob?", *The Guardian*, 2
October 2013.

"Women Shoulder the Responsibility of Unpaid Work", Office for National
Statistics, 19 November 2016, https://www.ons.gov.uk/employmentandla
bourmarket/peopleinwork/earningsandworkinghours/articles/womenshoulder
theresponsibilityofunpaidwork/2016-11-10#:~:text=Women%20carry%20out
%20an%20overall,to%20cooking%2C%20childcare%20and%20housework
(accessed 21 February 2024).

"Working for the Few: Political Capture and Economic Inequality", Oxfam
Briefing Paper 178, 20 January 2014.

Alesina, A. and Ardagna, S. "Tales of Fiscal Adjustment", *Economic Policy* 13,
no. 27, 1998: 489–545.

Alesina, A., Perotti, R., Tavares, J., Obstfeld, M., and Eichengreen, B. "The
Political Economy of Fiscal Adjustments", *Brookings Papers on Economic
Activity*, 1998.

Allegretti, A. and Elgot, J. "Covid: 'Greed' and Capitalism behind Vaccine
Success, Johnson Tells MPs", *The Guardian*, 24 March 2021.

Ambler, T. "Can we Trust Public Health England?", *Adam Smith Institute Blog*,
17 May 2022, https://www.adamsmith.org/blog/can-we-trust-public-health-en
gland (accessed 20 February 2024).

Austin, K. and Whannel, K. "Rishi Sunak Disappointed New Rail Strike Law
Not Used, Says No 10", *BBC News*, 29 January 2024, https://www.bbc.co.uk/
news/uk-politics-68131541 (accessed 28 February 2024).

Bateman, V. *The Sex Factor: How Women Made the West Rich* (London,
Polity, 2019).

Bateman, V., Gamage, D. K., Hengel, E., and Liu, X. "The Gender Imbalance
in UK Economics", Royal Economic Society, July 2021.

Beatty, C., Fothergill, S., and Powell, R. "Twenty Years on: Has the Economy
of the UK Coalfields Recovered?", *Environment and Planning A* 39, no. 7,
2007: 1654–1675.

Bharat-Ram, V. *Evolution of Economic Ideas: Smith to Sen and Beyond* (New
Delhi, Oxford University Press, 2017).

Blair, T. "We Won't Look Back to the 1970s", *The Times*, 31 March 1997.

Blinder, A. S., Canetti, E. R. D., Lebow, D. E., and Rudd, J. B. *Asking about Prices: A New Approach to Understanding Price Stickiness* (New York, Russell Sage Foundation, 1998).

Blyth, M. *Austerity: The History of a Dangerous Idea* (Oxford, Oxford University Press, 2018).

Boileau, B., Cribb, J., and Wernham, T. "Characteristics and Consequences of Families with Low Levels of Financial Wealth", Institute for Fiscal Studies, June 2023.

Brown, G. *"Labour Party and Political Change in Scotland, 1918–1929: The Politics of Five Elections"* (PhD thesis, University of Edinburgh, 1982).

Burgen. S. and Inman, P. "Spain Faces Crisis 'of Huge Proportions' over Unemployment and Banks", *The Guardian*, 27 April 2012.

Byrne, L. "'I'm Afraid There is no Money'. The Letter I Will Regret For Ever", *The Guardian*, 9 May 2015.

Carrington, D. "Microplastic Pollution Found near Summit of Mount Everest", *The Guardian*, 20 November 2020.

Cockett, R. *Thinking the Unthinkable: Think Tanks and the Economic Counter-Revolution 1931–1983* (London, Harper Collins, 1995).

Concerned Students of Economics 10, "An Open Letter to Greg Mankiw", *Harvard Political Review*, 2 November 2011, https://harvardpolitics.com/an-open-letter-to-greg-mankiw/ (accessed 29 February 2024).

Dasgupta, P. *Economics: A Very Short Introduction* (Oxford, Oxford University Press, 2007).

Davies, R. "Number of Problem Gamblers in the UK Rises to More than 400,000", *The Guardian*, 24 August 2017.

de Hoog, N. "'Unacceptable': How Raw Sewage Has Affected Rivers in England and Wales – in Maps", *The Guardian*, 12 September 2023, https://www.theguardian.com/environment/ng-interactive/2023/sep/12/unacceptable-how-raw-sewage-has-affected-rivers-in-england-and-wales-in-maps (accessed 28 February 2024).

Eagleton, T. *Why Marx was Right* (New Haven, Yale University Press, 2012).

Edwards, A. *Are We Rich Yet? The Rise of Mass Investment Culture in Contemporary Britain* (Oakland, University of California Press, 2022).

Elliott, L. "Greek Turmoil Offers George Osborne Justification for his Dictum of Austerity", *The Guardian*, 5 July 2015.

Fielder, E. "Emancipate Channel 4 from State Ownership", *Adam Smith Institute Press Release*, 4 April 2022, https://www.adamsmith.org/news/emancipate-channel-4-from-state-ownership (accessed 20 February 2024).

Fine, B. "Economic Imperialism and Intellectual Progress: The Present as History of Economic Thought?", *History of Economics Review* 32, no. 1, 2016: 10–35.

Fox, J. "The Comeback Keynes", *Time*, 27 January 2009.

Friedman, M. *Capitalism and Freedom* (Chicago, Chicago University Press, 1962).

Fulcher, J. *Capitalism: A Very Short Introduction* (Oxford, Oxford University Press, 2004).

Galbraith, J. K. *The Affluent Society* (London, Penguin, 1998).

Gallagher, J. and Robinson, R. "The Imperialism of Free Trade", *Economic History Review* 6, no. 1, 1953: 1–15.

Giddens, A. *Beyond Left and Right* (Cambridge, Polity, 1994).

Giddens, A. *The Third Way: The Renewal of Social Democracy* (Cambridge, Polity, 1998).

Grady, J. and Grocott, C., eds. *The Continuing Imperialism of Free Trade: Developments, Trends and the Role of Supranational Agents* (London, Routledge, 2019).

Graeber, D. *Bullshit Jobs: A Theory* (London, Penguin, 2018).

Greenwood, W. *Love on the Dole* (London, Jonathan Cape, 1974).

Grocott, C. and Grady, J. "'Naked Abroad': The Continuing Imperialism of Free Trade", *Capital and Class* 38, no. 3, 2014: 541–562.

Groves, J. "At Last! A True Tory Budget", *Daily Mail*, 24 September 2022.

Harari, D. "Productivity: Key Economic Indicators", House of Commons Library, 16 February 2024, https://commonslibrary.parliament.uk/research-briefings/sn02791/ (accessed 2 April 2024).

Hartwell, R. M. *A History of the Mont Pelerin Society* (Indianapolis, Liberty Fund Inc., 1995).

Harvey, D. *A Brief History of Neoliberalism* (Oxford, Oxford University Press, 2008).

Harvey, D. *A Companion to Marx's Capital: The Complete Edition* (London, Verso, 2018).

Hayek, F. A. *The Constitution of Liberty* (Chicago, Chicago University Press, 1960).

Hayek, F. A. *The Road to Serfdom* (London, Routledge, 1962).

Herndon, T., Ash, M., and Pollin, R. "Does High Public Debt Consistently Stifle Economic Growth? A Critique of Reinhart and Rogoff", Political Economy Research Institute Working Paper Series no. 322, April 2013.

Higham, N. "Cabinet Papers Reveal 'Secret Coal Pits Closure Plan'", *BBC News*, 3 January 2014, https://www.bbc.co.uk/news/uk-25549596 (accessed 2 April 2024).

Hill, R. and Myatt, T. *The Economics Anti-Textbook: A Critical Thinker's Guide to Microeconomics* (London, Zed Books, 2010).

Hobsbawm, E. *The Age of Revolutions: 1789–1848* (London, Abacus, 2005).

Inman, P. "Economics Students Aim to Tear up Free-Market Syllabus", *The Guardian*, 24 October 2013.

Johnson, B. "We Should be Humbly Thanking the Super-Rich, not Bashing Them", *Daily Telegraph*, 17 November 2013.

Johnson, E. and Moggridge, D., eds. *The Collected Writings of John Maynard Keynes*, 27 vols. (Cambridge, Cambridge University Press, 2012).

Kalms, Lord, "Ethics Boys", Letter to *The Times*, 8 March 2011.

Keen, S. *The New Economics: A Manifesto* (Cambridge, Polity, 2022).

Keep, M. "The Budget Deficit: A Short Guide", House of Commons Library, 15 January 2024.

Kelton, S. *The Deficit Myth: Modern Monetary Theory and How to Build a Better Economy* (London, John Murray, 2020).

Ketcham, C. "When Idiot Savants Do Climate Economics", *The Intercept*, 29 October 2023, https://theintercept.com/2023/10/29/william-nordhaus-climate-economics/ (accessed 14 February 2024).

Keynes, J. M. *A Tract on Monetary Reform* (London, Macmillan, 1923).

Keynes, J. M. *The General Theory of Employment, Interest and Money* (London, BN Publishing, 2008).

Kollewe, J. and Lawson, A. "Royal Mail Agrees upon Pay Deal with Postal Workers Union", *The Guardian*, 21 April 2023.

Krugman, P. "Review, Keynes: The Return of the Master by Robert Skidelsky", *The Guardian*, 30 August 2009.

Krugman, P. *Arguing with Zombies: Economics, Politics and the Fight for a Better Future* (New York, W. W. Norton and Company, 2020).

Litvin, D. *Empires of Profit: Commerce, Conquest, and Corporate Responsibility* (New York, Texere, 2003).

Malik, S. "Poundland Case: A Story we Couldn't Have Told Without Our Readers", *The Guardian*, 30 October 2013.

Mance, H. "Britain Has Had Enough of Experts, Says Gove", *Financial Times*, 3 June 2016.

Mankiw, N. G. "Know What You're Protesting", *New York Times*, 3 December 2011.

Manning, A. "Top Rate of Income Tax" (London, London School of Economics, Centre for Economic Performance, 2015), https://cep.lse.ac.uk/pubs/download/ea029.pdf (accessed 21 February 2024).

Mazzucato, M. *The Entrepreneurial State: Debunking Public vs Private Sector Myths* (London, Penguin, 2018).

Mazzucato, M. "Governing the Economics of the Common Good: From Correcting Market Failures to Shaping Collective Goals", *Journal of Economic Policy Reform* 27, no. 1, 2024: 1–24. doi:10.1080/17487870.2023.2280969.

McCraw, T. K. *Creating Modern Capitalism: How Entrepreneurs, Companies, and Countries Triumphed in Three Industrial Revolutions* (Cambridge, Massachusetts, Harvard University Press, 1997).

McDonnell, J. *Economics for the Many* (London, Verso, 2018).

McQuarrie, M. "Trump and the Revolt of the Rust Belt", *LSE Blog*, 11 November 2016, https://blogs.lse.ac.uk/usappblog/2016/11/11/23174/ (accessed 21 February 2024).

Mirowski, P. and Plehwe, D., eds. *The Road from Mont Pelerin: The Making of the Neoliberal Thought Collective* (Cambridge, Massachusetts, Harvard University Press, 2009).

Murray, A. et al. "Autism, Problematic Internet Use and Gaming Disorder: A Systematic Review", *Review Journal of Autism and Developmental Disorders* 9, no. 1, 2021: 120–140.

Neate, R. "Queen Finally Finds out Why no One Saw the Financial Crisis Coming", *The Guardian*, 13 December 2012.

Neate, R. "UK Millionaires Group Projects 'Tax our Wealth' on to Treasury and Bank of England", *The Guardian*, 21 November 2023.

Neate, R., Watt, N., and Elliott, L. "Royal Mail Shares Soar 38% as Labour Complains of Knockdown Price", *The Guardian*, 11 October 2013.

O'Carroll, L. "What is Causing the UK Crisis in Petrol Supplies?", *The Guardian*, 24 September 2021.

Offer, A. "The Market Turn: From Social Democracy to Market Liberalism", *The Economic History Review* 70, no. 4, 2017: 1051–1071.

Offer, A. and Soderberg, G. *The Nobel Factor: The Prize in Economics, Social Democracy and the Market Turn* (Princeton, New Jersey, Princeton University Press, 2016).

Orwell, G. "Review of the Road to Serfdom" in Orwell, S. and Angus, I., eds. *The Collected Essays, Journalism and Letters of George Orwell*, Vol. 3 (London, Penguin, 1982), 142–144.

Orwell, G. *The Road to Wigan Pier* (London, Penguin, 2001).

Paine, T. *The Rights of Man* (London, Everyman, 1966).

Pearce, R. *Attlee's Labour Governments, 1945–51* (London, Routledge, 1993).

Preston, K., Halpin, M., and Maguire, F. "The Black Pill: New Technology and the Male Supremacy of Involuntarily Celibate Men", *Men and Masculinities* 24, no. 5, 2021: 832–841.

Quinn, W. and Turner, J. D. *Boom and Bust: A Global History of Financial Bubbles* (Cambridge, Cambridge University Press, 2020).

Ramesh, R. "High-Stakes Gambling Machines 'Suck Money from Poorest Communities'", *The Guardian*, 4 January 2013.

Reich, R. "The State of Working America", *New York Times*, 4 September 2011.

Reinhart, C. and Rogoff, K. S. "Growth in a Time of Debt", National Bureau of Economic Research, Working Paper 15639, 2010.

Robinson, J. *Contributions to Modern Economics* (New York, Academic Press, 1978).

Robinson, R. "Non-European Foundations of European Imperialism: Sketch for a Theory of Collaboration", in Owen, R., ed. *Studies in the Theory of Imperialism* (London, Longman, 1972), 117–142.

Singer, P. *Marx: A Very Short Introduction* (Oxford, Oxford University Press, 2000).

Skidelsky, R. *John Maynard Keynes, 1883–1946: Economist, Philosopher, Statesman* (London, Penguin, 2003).

Skidelsky, R. *Keynes: The Return of the Master* (London, Penguin, 2009).

Skidelsky, R. *What's Wrong with Economics?: A Guide for the Perplexed* (New Haven, Yale University Press, 2021).

Smith, L. and Klemm, C. "Even as Behavioural Researchers We Couldn't Resist the Urge to Buy Toilet Paper", *The Guardian*, 5 March 2020.

Sparrow, A. "100 Quangos Abolished in Cost-Cutting Bonfire", *The Guardian*, 22 August 2012.

Stacey, K. "Liz Truss: Economic Consensus since 1997 to Blame for UK Woes – Not Me", *The Guardian*, 17 September 2023.

Starmer, K. "Voters Have Been Betrayed on Brexit and Immigration. I Stand Ready to Deliver", *Daily Telegraph*, 2 December 2023.

Stedman Jones, D. *Masters of the Universe: Hayek, Friedman, and the Birth of Neoliberal Politics* (Princeton, New Jersey, Princeton University Press, 2012).

Steil, B. *The Battle of Bretton Woods: John Maynard Keynes, Harry Dexter White and the Making of a New World Order* (Princeton, New Jersey, Princeton University Press, 2013).

Stratton, A. "Tory MP Philip Davies: Disabled People Could Work for Less Pay", *The Guardian*, 17 June 2011.

Syal, R. "What Options are Left for Rishi Sunak after Supreme Court's Rwanda Ruling?", *The Guardian*, 15 November 2023.

Taylor, F. W. *The Principles of Scientific Management* (Newark, New Jersey, Norton Library, 1967).

Taylor, F. W. *The Principles of Scientific Management* (London, Dover Publications, 2003).

Timmins, N. *The Five Giants: A Biography of the Welfare State* (London, Fontana Press, 1996).

Tooze, A. *Crashed: How a Decade of Financial Crises Changed the World* (London, Allen Lane, 2018).

Townsend, M. and Savage, M. "Fury as Braverman Depicts Homelessness as a 'Lifestyle Choice'", *The Guardian*, 4 November 2023.

Tran, M. "Union Leader Jack Jones Dies", *The Guardian*, 22 April 2009.

Trump, D. and Schwartz, T. *The Art of the Deal* (London, Arrow Books, 1987).

UK Parliament, Early Day Motions, "Formation of the Post-Crash Economics Society at Manchester University", EDM 641, 29 October 2013.

UK Parliament, Treasury Select Committee, "Treasury Committee Examines Impact of Russian Energy Sanctions and Effect on Cost of Living", 11 March 2022, https://committees.parliament.uk/committee/158/treasury-committee/news/161738/treasury-committee-examines-impact-of-russian-energy-sanctions-and-effect-on-cost-of-living/ (accessed 19 February 2024).

Unite the Union. "Unite Investigates: Profiteering across the Economy – It's Systemic", March 2023, https://www.unitetheunion.org/media/5442/profiteering-across-the-economy-march-2023.pdf (accessed 14 February 2024).

Varoufakis, Y. *Adults in the Room: My Battle with Europe's Deep Establishment* (London, The Bodley Head, 2017).

Wapshott, N. *Keynes Hayek: The Clash That Defined Modern Economics* (New York, W. W. Norton, 2011).

Watt, N. "David Cameron Beats a Hasty Retreat over Call for Voters to Pay Down Debts", *The Guardian*, 5 October 2011.

Wilcock, D. and Groves, J. "Rishi Sunak Lashes out at 'Ideological' Eco-Zealots Who 'Don't Care about Families' as he Comes out Swinging to Defend Green U-Turn Saying Brits Should not be Hit with £15,000 Cost of New Cars,

Boilers and Eco-Taxes Earlier than the Rest of the World", *Daily Mail*, 21 September 2023 (accessed 4 April 2024).

Wintour, P. and Watt, N. "David Cameron to Urge Households to Pay off Debts", *The Guardian*, 5 October 2011.

Woodhouse, J. "Fixed Odds Betting Terminals", 2019, Briefing Paper, House of Commons Library.

Wren-Lewis, S. *The Lies we were Told: Politics, Economics, Austerity and Brexit* (Bristol, Bristol University Press, 2018).

Yueh, L. *The Great Economists: How Their Ideas Can Help us Today* (London, Viking, 2018).

Yueh, L. *The Great Crashes: Lessons from Global Meltdowns and How to Prevent Them* (London, Penguin, 2023).

INDEX

Printed in the United States
by Baker & Taylor Publisher Services